# GOING PRIVATE

# STATE OF HEALTH SERIES

Edited by Chris Ham, Fellow in Health Policy and Management, King's Fund College in London

*Current and forthcoming titles*

*Financing Health Care in the 1990s*
John Appleby

*Patients, Policies and Politics*
John Butler

*Going Private*
Michael Calnan, Sarah Cant and Jonathan Gabe

*Public Law and Health Service Accountability*
Diane Longley

*Hospitals in Transition*
Tim Packwood, Justin Keen and Martin Buxton

*Planned Markets and Public Competition*
Richard B. Saltman and Casten von Otter

*Whose Standards?*
Charlotte Williamson

# GOING PRIVATE
Why People Pay for their
Health Care

**Michael Calnan, Sarah Cant
and Jonathan Gabe**

**Open University Press**
Buckingham · Philadelphia

Open University Press
Celtic Court
22 Ballmoor
Buckingham
MK18 1XW

and
1900 Frost Road, Suite 101
Bristol, PA 19007, USA

First Published 1993

A catalogue record of this book is available from the British Library

0 335 09980 7 (Paperback)      0 335 09981 5 (Hardback)

*Library of Congress Cataloging-in-Publication Data*

Calnan, Michael
    Going private : changing expectations about health care? / Michael
Calnan, Sarah Cant, and Jonathan Gabe.
        p.      cm. – (State of health series)
    Includes bibliographical references and index.
    ISBN 0–335–09981–5   ISBN 0–335–09980–7 (pbk.)
    1. Insurance, Health – Great Britain.   2. National Health Service
(Great Britain).   3. Medical care – Great Britain – Public opinion.
I. Cant, Sarah, 1965–      .   II. Gabe, Jonathan.   III. Title.
IV. Series.
RA395.G6C35   1993
362.1′0941 – dc20                                            92–40057
                                                                CIP

Typeset by Type Study, Scarborough
Printed in Great Britain by St Edmundsbury Press Ltd,
Bury St Edmunds, Suffolk

# CONTENTS

# SERIES EDITOR'S INTRODUCTION

Health services in many developed countries have come under critical scrutiny in recent years. In part this is because of increasing expenditure, much of it funded from public sources, and the pressure this has put on governments seeking to control public spending. Also important has been the perception that resources allocated to health services are not always deployed in an optimal fashion. Thus at a time when the scope for increasing expenditure is extremely limited, there is a need to search for ways of using existing budgets more efficiently. A further concern has been the desire to ensure access to health care of various groups on an equitable basis. In some countries this has been linked to a wish to enhance patient choice and to make service providers more responsive to patients as 'consumers'.

Underlying these specific concerns are a number of more fundamental developments which have a significant bearing on the performance of health services. Three are worth highlighting. First, there are demographic changes, including the ageing population and the decline in the proportion of the population of working age. These changes will both increase the demand for health care and at the same time limit the ability of health services to respond to this demand.

Second, advances in medical science will also give rise to new demands within the health services. These advances cover a range of possibilities, including innovations in surgery, drug therapy, screening and diagnosis. The pace of innovation is likely to quicken as the end of the century approaches, with significant implications for the funding and provision of services.

Third, public expectations of health services are rising as those who use services demand higher standards of care. In part, this is stimulated by developments within the health service, including the availability of new technology. More fundamentally, it stems from the emergence of a more educated and informed population, in which people are accustomed to being treated as consumers rather than patients.

Against this background, policymakers in a number of countries are reviewing the future of health services. Those countries which have traditionally relied on a market in health care are making greater use of regulation and planning. Equally, those countries which have traditionally relied on regulation and planning are moving towards a more competitive approach. In no country is there complete satisfaction with existing methods of financing and delivery, and everywhere there is a search for new policy instruments.

The aim of this series is to contribute to debate about the future of health services through an analysis of major issues in health policy. These issues have been chosen because they are both of current interest and of enduring importance. The series is intended to be accessible to students and informed lay readers as well as to specialists working in this field. The aim is to go beyond a textbook approach to health policy analysis and to encourage authors to move debate about their issue forward. In this sense, each book presents a summary of current research and thinking, and an exploration of future policy directions.

Dr Chris Ham
Fellow in Health Policy and Management
King's Fund College

# PREFACE AND ACKNOWLEDGEMENTS

Since the inception of the NHS there has always been a private health sector in the United Kingdom, although its size has varied according to political, economic and social circumstances. The important question about why some people still 'need' a private acute sector, given that they also pay for NHS care, has been neglected, at least until recently. Sociological research has tended to focus on 'problems' associated with patterns of 'overutilization' or 'underutilization' of public health services. Of late this has changed and the private sector has become the focus of interest for researchers and policy makers. There are many reasons for this increase in interest but one of them is clearly due to the increase in the size of the private sector encouraged by the growth in the coverage of private health insurance among the UK population, or at least certain sectors of it.

This book is about the growth in private health insurance and is based on an empirical study carried out in the South East of England in the late 1980s when private health insurance subscription was reaching new heights. It is about why some people subscribe to it, why and when they use it and what value they place on it. While we have employed both survey and qualitative methods we have also attempted to illustrate the value of qualitative methods for this particular research question.

This book would never have reached completion without the support of a number of organizations and individuals. We would particularly like to thank the Economic and Social Research Council for funding the study. Thanks also go to Professor Louis Opit for his help with setting up the study; to the respondents for spending so much time in the interviews, and to the general practitioners who helped to identify the sample. Finally, we are

very grateful to Jackie Newton and Linda McDonnell for typing
various drafts of manuscripts and to Barbara Wall for help with the
data processing.

# 1

# INTRODUCTION

The funding and organization of health care in the United Kingdom has never been far from the political agenda since the inception of the National Health Service (NHS) in 1948. With the recent health service reforms, however, it has become a major political issue. One of the focuses of this controversy has been the privatization of health care and the extent to which it has challenged or 'undermined' the NHS. Privatization has taken a number of different forms (Mohan, 1991) but a key feature has been the expansion of the private health-care acute sector. While there has always been such private health care alongside the NHS, its size has varied according to political, social and economic circumstances. In recent years the proportion of the population covered by health insurance has been at its highest since the introduction of the NHS. Indeed, the vast majority of people who use private health-care acute services now have private insurance coverage.

Such an increase in private health insurance raises a number of very important questions. For example, why do people subscribe to private insurance schemes given the availability of a national health service? When and why do they use it once they have taken out a subscription? And what do they think of private health care compared with NHS care? To date, this range of questions has rarely been addressed by researchers, with most limiting themselves to attitude surveys about the relative merits of public and private health care. In the following pages we shall attempt to answer these questions in turn, drawing primarily on evidence from a recently completed in-depth interview study about the knowledge, beliefs and experience of health care of people who either have or do not have private health insurance.

In this introductory chapter, however, we shall try to place the private health-care insurer and user in a historical and social context. More specifically, we want to examine the nature of the changes in private health insurance over the last four decades and offer some explanations for these changes.

## DEVELOPMENTS IN THE PRIVATE HEALTH-CARE SECTOR SINCE 1948

Evidence that private medicine has been growing since the creation of the NHS comes from two sources: the increased number of subscribers to private health insurance and the rising numbers of private hospitals and hospital beds. It is very difficult to pinpoint whether increases in private health insurance subscriptions produced an increase in hospital beds or vice versa. They are clearly related and interdependent, although more so now than they were in the early years of the NHS when access to private health care was not dependent on insurance cover, and private hospital bills were frequently settled by patients themselves. Indeed, as recently as 1975, 40 per cent of such bills were still paid for by patients rather than the insurance companies. By 1989, however, this proportion had fallen to 30 per cent and half of these were overseas patients (Laing and Buisson, 1990).

In the early years, immediately after the introduction of the NHS, the future of private medicine was uncertain and it was commonly assumed that people would not be willing to pay for something that was available 'free of charge' (Higgins, 1988). During the 1950s, however, subscriptions to the three insurance companies that dominated the market, British United Provident Association (BUPA), Private Patients Plan (PPP) and the Western Provident Association (WPA) began to show a modest but steady increase. Thus, between 1955 and 1965, the proportion of the population insured with these companies increased from 1.2 per cent to 2.7 per cent. This pattern continued until the mid-1970s when a temporary decline in overall subscriptions occurred. In 1974, 4.2 per cent of the population were insured: by 1977 it had dropped to 4 per cent.

Between 1979 and 1981, however, the private insurance market improved dramatically, with the percentage insured increasing from 5 per cent to 7.3 per cent (Laing and Buisson, 1990). This upsurge stemmed mainly from an increase in schemes provided by employers. Thereafter, the rate of growth fell back to the pre-1970 level (Higgins, 1992), although evidence from the insurers for 1988–89 points to another upsurge in subscriptions, with numbers increasing by about 9 per cent over the year – the highest annual growth rate since the boom of 1979–81 (Laing and Buisson, 1990). Thus, according to the Association of British Insurers, 13 per cent of the population were insured in 1989. However, recent newspaper reports suggest that since mid-1991 the percentage of the population covered by private health insurance has started to fall again, mainly as a result of a sharp increase in the cost of premiums (Fraser, 1991; Hughes, 1991). Even so, the increase in subscriptions since the Conservatives came to power in 1979 has been noteworthy – a point which is underlined when one realizes that these figures refer to net increases in subscriptions and do not record the relatively high number of ex-subscribers who have let their subscriptions lapse.

Given the number of company purchase schemes during the 1970s and early 1980s it is not surprising that the majority of currently insured are in such schemes. Data from the *General Household Survey* (OPCS, 1989) indicate that in 1987 54 per cent of the insured were in company schemes, with the remainder in individual (24 per cent) or group schemes (18 per cent). However, it seems that recently the picture has begun to change with net individual subscriber numbers beginning to grow, due in part to aggressive marketing and careful targeting by insurers and an increase in disposable income amongst those groups who have traditionally been insured (Higgins, 1992). This growth slowed down in 1991 because of the combined effects of the recession and higher premiums (Laing and Buisson, 1992).

As might be expected, those who have private health insurance tend to have professional and managerial jobs. Thus, the percentage of people aged 45–64 in professional occupations who were covered by private health insurance in 1987 was 34 per cent, compared with 3 per cent of skilled manual workers and 2 per cent of unskilled manual workers (OPCS, 1989). Moreover, given the marked regional variation in coverage, the figure is probably higher for those professionals who live in or around the London area where many of the consultancy and financial firms who offer company-based schemes are based. In 1987, for inner and outer London combined, the proportion of the population covered was 29 per cent, compared with 7 per cent in the North West, 3 per cent in the North and 4 per cent both in Wales and Scotland. This variation in part reflects differences in disposable income and the unequal distribution of 'benefits in kind'. However, it may also reflect a decision on the part of insurers not to expand into the working-class market because these potential subscribers are deemed to be a bad risk and/or high-cost patients.

There are also variations in coverage and subscription by gender, marital status, age and ethnicity. Considerably more men than women hold insurance policies but roughly equal numbers of both sexes are actually covered. Thus, while 11 per cent of married men held policies in 1987 compared with only 2 per cent of married women, this gender imbalance was corrected as a result of the number of such women (10 per cent) who were covered by their partner (OPCS, 1989). The pattern is similar although less marked for single people, with 7 per cent of single men holding policies compared with 4 per cent of single women. Policy holding and coverage also varies by age with the highest coverage being in the middle-age range (45–64). As regards ethnicity, the limited evidence available suggests that private health insurance is restricted to whites. Those black people who use private medicine – usually a private consultation with a general practitioner – pay out of their own pockets (Thorogood, 1992).

Our second measure of the growth of private medicine concerns hospitals and hospital beds. Since 1979 there has been a spectacular increase in both these areas, with private hospitals increasing by 39 per cent and private bed numbers by 58 per cent (Independent Hospitals Association, 1989). While some of this increase in beds has been in areas poorly served by the NHS such as abortions, open-heart surgery and alcohol and drug rehabilitation, expansion has also occurred in the area of acute hospital services where the NHS provides an alternative. For example, between 1982 and 1988 the total number of acute beds in the private sector increased by almost a quarter (CSO, 1991). This expansion of acute services is particularly significant as it resulted in the private sector treating 16.7 per cent of all cases of elective surgery in 1986 compared with 13.2 per cent in 1981 (Nicholl *et al.*, 1989a). Moreover the proportion of operations carried out privately in 1986 for conditions such as arthritis of the hip was even higher. This growth in private hospital beds and treatments should also be seen against a background of a fall in the number of available beds in NHS hospitals over the same period (CSO, 1991).

Similarly, although pay beds accounted for less than 2 per cent of all acute beds in 1989, there is evidence of a recent increase in pay-bed authorizations, possibly because Health Authorities see them as an important source of revenue. Between 1981 and 1989 the number of pay-bed authorizations for in-patient care gradually increased from 27 000 to 30 000, although this still compares unfavourably with 1971 when the figure was 44 000 (CSO, 1991).

Despite this apparent growth in the private acute sector perhaps the most important change has been in the pattern of hospital ownership. While 29 per cent of private beds were in commercial hands in 1979 this proportion had increased to 56 per cent by 1989, with the remainder in religious or charitable non-profit making hospitals (Busfield, 1992). A crucial stimulus for this change was the involvement of multinational corporations, mainly from the USA, who invested heavily in hospitals in the late 1970s to meet the growth in private health insurance (Rayner, 1987). Recently, however, there have been radical changes within the for-profit sector itself with two of the leading US groups selling up as a result of falling profits at home. At the same time, two new European companies have taken a stake in the UK market (Higgins, 1992).

In sum, then, private medicine has grown considerably since the NHS was established. There has not only been a substantial increase in the number of subscribers to private health insurance but also a similar expansion in the number of private hospitals and hospital beds. But why have such developments taken place? We shall turn to this question next.

## EXPLANATIONS FOR THE EXPANSION OF THE PRIVATE HEALTH-CARE MARKET

Much of the debate about why private health care has expanded in recent years is concerned with whether it has been as a result of the actions of providers or in response to consumer demand. We shall consider each in turn.

### The role of providers

Supply-side arguments concentrate on the actions of the state, and those of the private insurance companies, the private hospitals and the medical profession, both hospital doctors and general practitioners. Of these, the state is perhaps the key actor and can support the provision of private health care either through the expansion of private pay beds in NHS hospitals, or by encouraging the growth of the independent private health-care sector. In some respects the Conservative Government from 1979 onwards pursued both these policies, although with more emphasis on the latter.

Somewhat ironically, however, it was the previous Labour administration which had provided the initial stimulus for growth in the private sector by deciding to phase out pay beds from the NHS, thus giving private suppliers an incentive to fill the gap (Higgins, 1988). Moreover, the introduction by Labour of an incomes policy (the Social Contract) in 1976–7 encouraged employers and latterly some trade unions to arrange private health insurance for their employees and members as a payment in kind, and this too had the effect of expanding the private health-care market.

Consequently, when the Conservatives came to office in 1979, private medicine was already growing. This was further encouraged by the introduction of a series of important policy changes which Mohan and Woods (1985) have summarized. First, the Health Services Act, which the Conservatives introduced in 1980, contained a number of provisions designed to reduce the restrictions on private health care. The Health Service Board set up under Labour to facilitate the phasing out of pay beds was abolished and the Secretary of State re-authorized to approve the use of NHS facilities for paying patients. As a result, the reduction in the number of pay beds was reversed and controls on private hospital development relaxed. Moreover, District Health Authorities were encouraged to contract with private hospitals for the first time.

Second, the Conservatives relaxed the Town and Country Planning legislation in order to avoid 'unjustified' restrictions on hospital development. This made it easier for new hospitals to be built regardless of the impact on the local community, with profitability becoming the chief concern in planning decisions. Third, introducing the Finance Act 1981 increased the attractiveness of private health insurance by making insurance premiums paid by employers on behalf of employees and by lower paid workers with individual subscriptions tax deductible. This increased the coverage of company-run schemes. The Act also facilitated the raising of capital for small-scale entrepreneurial activity through the Small Business Start-up Scheme. Finally, the Conservative Government changed consultant contracts, with full-timers being allowed for the first time to earn up to 10 per cent of their NHS salary from private practice and maximum part-timers being required to forego less of their NHS salary (one-eleventh instead of two-elevenths) while being allowed to undertake as much private practice as they wished. As a result the amount of private practice such doctors were able to undertake without forfeiting NHS privileges increased dramatically and, as Higgins points out (1988, p. 87), 'meant that in 1984 there were many more consultant staff available, willing and eager to do private practice than there had been in 1979 . . . the potential for the expansion of private practice was dramatically changed'.

Conservative Government policies in the early 1980s therefore created the necessary conditions for the rapid growth in the private hospitals and beds and in insurance cover which, as we have seen, took place in their first term in office. But why were these policies pursued?

One possible explanation is that they were driven by ideological conviction, and in particular by neo-liberalism which makes up one of the main strands of New Right ideology (Flynn, 1989). This ideology, which is based on a belief in self-reliance, individual responsibility and the market, is essentially hostile to a Welfare State built on a 'social equity model'. The latter is premised on the idea that health care is allocated according to need rather than demand and that scarce resources are rationed by providers according to unspecified criteria (Klein, 1982). It also places great emphasis on the value of equality and its achievement through centralization and the public ownership of the means of production. Providers in this context are paid directly by the state, usually through salaries (Klein, 1982).

Neo-liberalism, by comparison, places its faith in the 'market economy model' and consumer choice as a means of allocating care. Emphasis is placed on freedom of action and personal responsibility and state involvement is rejected because it is perceived to constrain such freedom and create dependency. Thus, it is believed that if people are offered state benefits such as health care it weakens their desire to look after themselves and erodes their moral wellbeing and voluntary expression of social concern. On this view, charity rather than the state is seen as the proper vehicle to meet social problems (Green, 1985).

The mechanisms through which such freedom and personal responsibility are pursued and achieved are private ownership and rewards. Health care is seen as part of the reward system and as a result, access to health care is determined largely by the ability to pay. Likewise, providers of care are directly rewarded according to market forces mainly through fee for service payments (Klein, 1982). Hence, in this approach, the consumer is sovereign and health care is based on demand expressed through the market, whereas in the 'social equity model' health care is based on need, with resources being distributed centrally on grounds of equity.

Those who argue that health care is best funded through the market see the market model having a number of advantages which reflect the assumption that health care is a commodity like any other commodity. It is claimed to have the following advantages: it is more responsive to consumer preferences, contributing to innovation and equal treatment; rationing by price is a fairer system of meeting need than rationing in other ways; it is more flexible and brings about a large expansion of hospital-based services; it removes bureaucratic inefficiency, involves greater consumer and provider responsibility and stimulates levels of social welfare expenditure (Harris and Seldon, 1977; Hindess, 1989).

As has often been remarked, this brand of New Right ideology has been very influential amongst Conservatives since they returned to power in 1979 and has facilitated many of the changes in health-care provision (Flynn, 1989; Harrison *et al.*, 1990). However, the continuing existence of a publicly-funded NHS alongside the private sector suggests that the Government has been held back from implementing a full-blooded neo-liberal approach. Why should this be so?

Arguably the main reason for the Conservatives continuing to insist that the NHS is 'safe in our hands' is political. They have lacked both the popular and professional support for instituting a totally privately funded health-care system, and have had to bow to pressure to maintain a mixed economy of welfare. For instance, throughout the 1980s the Welfare State in general and the NHS in particular has retained its popularity amongst all social and political groupings and there is evidence of increased support over the decade for more spending on health and other welfare services, even among supporters of the Conservative Government (Taylor-Gooby, 1991a). At the same time, however, there is a high level of support for the existence of private medicine outside the NHS and increasing dissatisfaction with the quality of the service provided by the NHS itself. Such ambivalence – recognizing the advantages of the private sector while continuing to support the Welfare State – can be explained in a number of ways. For Taylor-Gooby (1987), support for both public and private sectors is explained by self-interest. On this argument people derive their rather narrow and individualistic perceptions of interests from capitalist ideology. Under capitalism, goods and services become private property, so that what are really social relations (e.g. production and consumption of health care) become experienced as exchange relations. Attention is focused on the exchange of things as 'values'. Individual purchase of a good is continually legitimated as the normal way to conduct social relations, and self-interest is to do with the capacity to command goods. Thus there is an in-built prejudice in favour of private provision because it is a market relation. At the same time, the principle of maximizing command over goods produces an interest in favour of the use of state collective services, where those offer a good deal. Thus there is support for the state service because it is beneficial but the public assert the legitimacy of the market since this is the basis of consumption in our society. Exit from the Welfare State and support for the private sector depends on the balance of state and private provision. The lack of subsidies to the private sector, however, limits enrolment and yet the nature of capitalism ensures support for market principles and privatization. Therefore, self-interest ensures support for both the state and the market and a belief that the private sector offers better facilities is not in opposition to support for state services.

Saunders and Harris (1989), in contrast, interpret ambivalence in a different way, as an artefact of the structure of social provision. People appear to support both the public and private sectors because they are 'trapped consumers'. They support the public sector because they are forced to pay taxes and therefore want a good service. But they also support the private sector because they see this as their ideal preference, meeting their 'need' for self-assertion, autonomy and control. On this argument, then, the reason for people's ambivalence is the lack of choice offered by the state, not the choice offered by the market as Taylor-Gooby would argue. Thus, these writers approach the issue of ambivalence from opposing standpoints, emphasizing either provider- or consumer-led explanations.

Whatever the reasons for this ambivalence (and we return to this issue in Chapter 3 and offer our own interpretation) the consequence for the Government has been double edged. On the one hand it has prevented it from following neo-liberal orthodoxy to the letter and replacing the NHS with a privately funded system. On the other hand, it has given it the confidence to make the policy changes which have facilitated the growth of the private sector alongside public provision.

At the same time, the nature of these changes has also been influenced by the reactions of those working in the NHS itself. Encouragement for the expansion of the private sector has been received from those segments of the medical profession who have stood to gain financially from such developments. Thus the Conservatives' plans have been endorsed by hospital consultants who have been the major beneficiaries of the growth in medical fees paid out by insurance companies in recent years. According to Klein (1989) such fees increased from £37 million to over £200 million between 1979 and 1987. This in turn reflects the increasing number of NHS consultants undertaking at least some private work – estimated at 85 per cent in 1984 (Griffith *et al.*, 1985), the highest proportion since the NHS came into being. It also means that if the increased fees were spread evenly across the consultant body it would represent an average income from private practice in 1987 of almost £17 000 (Klein, 1989). In reality, however, such income is likely to be heavily skewed, with surgeons in particular earning well above this average whereas others like geriatricians are likely to have benefited far less from the liberalization of consultant contracts. Furthermore, some of these consultants have also made money out of their ownership, wholly or in part, of the new private hospitals, having invested in the Government's Business Expansion Scheme in order to benefit from the substantial tax relief which it allows (Higgins, 1988).

Junior hospital doctors, on the other hand, are less likely to have been enthusiastic about the growth of the private sector, given the burdens that have traditionally been imposed on them as a result of their consultants' involvement in private health care. For instance, it has been reported that juniors have been asked by their consultants to contravene their contractual obligations to the NHS and assist at operations in private hospitals, while also having to shoulder a heavier burden on NHS wards as their superiors are away undertaking their private practice (Higgins, 1988). As far as the Government is concerned, however, the views of such doctors are likely to have been considered inconsequential because of their relative lack of political power and their reluctance to speak out because of the way in which their careers depend on the patronage of their superiors (Allen, 1988).

The attitude of general practitioners is also likely to have had little bearing on Government policy towards private health care to date because of their limited involvement in this sector (Butler and Calnan, 1987). However, they may have played a role in restricting the impact of these policy changes because of their apparent reluctance to refer patients to private practitioners, in part perhaps because of the lack of financial reimbursement. Thus Gillam (1985) found that general practitioner (GP) referrals to private consultants were twice as likely to be initiated by patients as NHS referrals. On the other hand GP involvement in private practice may increase as a result of the recent Government reforms of the health service. Already, GP budget holders have found politically lucrative legal loopholes which allow them to syphon off NHS funds to their own private medical companies and sell surgical services back to themselves (Ferriman, 1991). Also, their purchasing role may put them in an even more powerful position in terms of the private sector.

It would seem, then, that it is the hospital consultants who have been most encouraging and have had the most to gain from the Government's policy on private health care. At the same time, however, it could be argued that these consultants' and their GP counterparts' continuing support for the NHS has limited the Government's scope for developing a totally privately funded health-care system. It is certainly the case that there has been intense professional opposition to the creation of NHS trusts, the new GP contracts and the introduction of GP budget holders (Haines and Iliffe, 1992; Loveridge and Starkey, 1992), partly on the grounds that these represent the privatization of the service from within. On the other hand, the fact that the Conservatives failed to consult the profession before introducing these changes suggests that we should be wary of overstating the power of medicine to influence the development of health policy (Elston, 1991).

Besides these political considerations we would argue that the state's policy towards private medicine has also been motivated by economic concerns. First, like all governments in developed countries, the Conservatives have been faced with persistent upward pressure on health spending due to demographic changes, the cost of new technologies and rising public expectations (Allsop, 1984). At the same time, they have been faced with a reduction in income as a result of a series of economic crises over which they have presided. Faced with such financial pressures the Government's response has been to argue along monetarist lines that an open-ended commitment to the Welfare State is unaffordable. It is said to impose an excessive burden on industry and divert resources from the 'productive' to the 'unproductive' sector of the economy (Mohan, 1986). Given this assessment the solution has been to reduce the public-sector borrowing requirement and turn to the private sector as a way of supplementing the state's limited resources (Mohan, 1991). It is partly for this reason that the policy changes impacting on the private health-care sector were introduced in the early 1980s.

Second, these changes have also been introduced in order to maximize the opportunities of small and large business for capital accumulation (Mohan, 1991). Thus the abolition of the Health Services Board, the introduction of the Finances Act and changes to the Town and Country Planning legislation have enhanced the ability of potential private hospital developers to raise capital for their projects and obtain the necessary planning permission. The resulting private hospital development has also benefited the medical supply companies whose market for products ranging from high technology equipment and medical information systems to food and linen has increased significantly.

Instituting policies that have facilitated growth has not been without problems for the private sector, however. For example, the abolition of controls over private hospital development has been one of the main reasons for the recent overcapacity in this sector. There was a spurt in hospital building in the early 1980s which subsequently led to a dramatic increase in hospital beds, especially in the four Thames Regional Health Authorities (Rayner, 1987). This in turn resulted in an oversupply of beds and low occupancy levels (Mohan and Woods, 1985). In 1986 occupancy levels were just 57 per cent nationally and 52 per cent in London, somewhat below the 60 per cent break-even point (Laing and Buisson, 1990). For hospitals run by religious organizations, the level was even lower at 39 per cent (Nicholl *et al.*, 1989b).

The changes have also attracted the influx of for-profit companies, thereby making the market much more competitive. As Higgins (1992) has noted, private hospital corporations, particularly from the USA, appeared to believe that with the return of the Conservatives in 1979 and the policy changes they introduced, the private sector in the UK was now 'ripe for expansion'. The result was a growing 'corporatization' of private hospital provision with the not-for-profit companies increasingly being swallowed up by the US investor-owned for-profit corporations. Those UK companies that were left in turn reacted critically, accusing the Americans of contributing to the growing problem of overbedding and causing the spiralling cost of private treatment in their drive to maximize profits (Higgins, 1988).

By the late 1980s it was clear that the fortunes of the private-sector hospitals had turned and a process of rationalization got under way. As we noted earlier, the majority of US multinationals sold up, resulting in three commercial companies, two UK (BUPA Hospitals and Nuffield Hospital) and one US (AMI), controlling two-fifths of the market in 1989 (Busfield, 1992).

At the same time, private hospitals have had to face increased competition from the NHS as a result of Health Authorities being allowed to re-introduce pay beds without being forced to charge their full economic cost (Mohan, 1986). This has been particularly marked in the South East of England where there was already overcapacity in the private sector. Furthermore, the creation of NHS Hospital Trusts in the recent health service reforms is likely to stimulate the further growth of NHS pay-bed facilities as these hospitals consider their options for revenue generation (Laing and Buisson, 1990).

Nor have the problems been restricted to private hospitals. Expansion has also created difficulties for the insurance companies. While tax concessions to employers greatly increased the number of employer-paid subscribers, it also resulted in an increase in claims, as these subscribers were from a wider range of socio-economic groups with higher rates of morbidity, and tended to maximize their use of services because their insurance had been given as a perk (Higgins, 1988).

In addition, the growth in the market has resulted in increased competition between insurance companies and the proliferation of insurance schemes. Thus it was reported that there were 28 private health insurers in the UK market by 1991, with BUPA's market share having fallen from 80 per cent in the 1970s to under 50 per cent in 1990 (Hughes, 1991). Initially it had lost ground to the other two providents, WPA and PPP, with the latter increasing its market share from 25 per cent in 1985 to 29 per cent in 1990. In 1990 WPA's share stood at 7 per cent. Recently, however, all the provident associations have been under threat from commercial companies such as the Norwich Union and Sun Alliance. The latter have undercut the provident schemes and, through massive advertising campaigns, have increased their market share to 11 per cent.

At the same time BUPA's losses have mounted. It reported its first loss in 1981 and a record loss of £63 million in 1990, mainly as a result of trying to keep premiums down to remain competitive (Hughes, 1991). This has led BUPA to increase its premiums on average by 20 per cent in 1991, although insurers throughout the industry have increased their premiums by an average 18 per cent over the same period because of low profits due to increased competition (Boliver, 1991). However, premiums have also been increased to cover mounting claims and spiralling medical costs, particularly the costs of high technology medicine. Fees paid to surgeons, anaesthetists and physicians amounted to £480 million in 1990 (Laing and Buisson, 1992).

It is interesting to note in this context that at the same time as private health insurers use the rhetoric of 'choice' as a selling point, they are now beginning to identify the problem of the 'abuse' of private medical cover. According to a spokesman from PPP, 'Because private medical cover is perceived as free at the point of sale it is often abused . . . We are trying to make clients understand that the more they claim, the more their premiums will rise' (quoted in Boliver, 1991).

Not surprisingly, with the increased competition between insurance companies there has been a proliferation of insurance schemes, particularly the growth of cheaper policies (budget plans) and plans targeted at the over-sixty year olds (the group which was allowed tax relief on premiums in the Budget of 1990). The most costly plans (*Which*, 1991) are the standard policies which cover the widest range of treatment and are more likely to meet hospitals' and doctors' bills in full. There is a marked variation in the price of premiums but the minimum cost is seldom less than £400 per year for a married couple in their late thirties with two children. For example, the BUPA care plan which does not cover either existing health problems or surgeons' and anaesthetists' bills would cost a couple in their thirties with two children between £685 and £1399 per year in 1991. The BUPA budget plan would cost the same family £427 per year, although it does not cover outpatient treatment and existing health problems and has a limit of £15 000 that it will pay for each person within a policy year. Thus, the budget plans are significantly cheaper but the cover is much reduced. A popular version is a 'waiting list' policy where the insurance pays for private medicine only if the NHS cannot treat your condition within six weeks.

Some of the policies also cover access to the NHS and if the NHS is used instead of a private hospital most plans pay a cash benefit from £20 to £105 per night depending on the plan. This covers hospital costs as well as additional costs. Thus, NHS pay beds are also covered under some of the insurance plans.

It would seem, then, that there is considerable variation in cover in terms of hospital care, i.e. hospital bills, outpatient care, doctors' and anaesthetists' fees and the ceiling on size of payment. The most expensive plans do guarantee to meet the full cost of a hospital stay and all the bills associated with the treatment. However, with most other policies there is the problem of whether the cover will be adequate.

Previously it was shown that the growth in the private health sector had occurred specifically in the area of acute elective surgery. Thus, health insurance coverage is usually restricted to this area and seldom includes treatment for Aids and related conditions, normal pregnancy and childbirth, treatment on kidney machines, private treatment from GPs, dentists and opticians, treatment for conditions such as alcoholism and psychiatric disorders and treatment for long-term illnesses such as multiple sclerosis.

In addition to these restrictions some plans do not immediately cover health problems which started before the plan was taken out, but automatically include them after a period without further treatment. With other plans, existing problems will usually be permanently excluded. Also plans usually run for a year and insurance companies guarantee renewal for as long as required. However, more recently, some plans have been introduced which are not automatically renewable and this can cause problems if there is a medical history. In such cases it may be difficult to switch plans.

In some ways employers and their employees have been particularly advantaged by the increased competition in the insurance market in that, as premiums rise, they can shop around for the 'best buy', especially from the new entrants to the market. The big household name companies have been in a particularly strong position in this respect as they are also targets for the new insurance companies who need their custom to gain credibility. Certainly, with rising premiums for employers their relationship with the insurance companies has become critical, as their sensitivity to price increases and subscription costs can create a volatility in the market place which shapes significantly the nature of the service.

In sum, then, the growth of the private health-care market over the last decade has been influenced by the actions of providers and, in particular, by the state. The Conservative Government, influenced by New Right ideology and monetarist economics has developed a series of policies which have facilitated this expansion, although it has been constrained in its attempts to introduce a totally privately funded system by both popular and professional support for the NHS.

It may well be that current Government initiatives such as providing tax relief on private health insurance for the over-sixties in the Budget of April 1990 and eliminating the remaining restrictions on private hospital development in the NHS and Community Care Act 1990 may facilitate further expansion of the private market. However, as we have seen, deregulation has also produced competition and instability for private insurance companies and private hospitals, with rising premiums and falling profits. Moreover, recent NHS reforms such as the introduction of independent hospital trusts and GP fundholding may increase the competition between the NHS and the private sector for those who want what private medicine has to offer. As a result the prospects for the providers of private health care remain uncertain.

Whatever the behaviour of providers and its implications for private health care, however, such a focus can only give us a partial understanding of recent and future developments. The user's or consumer's perspective also needs to be considered. We shall therefore turn to this next.

**The role of the consumer**

At the outset it should be noted that the very notion of a health care 'consumer' is problematic. Unlike consumers of other commodities those seeking medical care are constrained by their lack of knowledge of the choices available and are dependent on professional expertise, especially in life-threatening situations. The intrinsically unequal nature of the relationship means that they are not in a position to shop around for the best buy and make informed choices as those who advocate a business model of health care assume (Allsop, 1992; Flynn, 1992). Moreover, the distinction between the consumer and the producer of health care is not as clear-cut as some might think, as ordinary people are also responsible for producing good health and preventing illness (Stacey, 1976).

At the same time, however, it is the case that one of the major objectives of recent Government policy has been precisely to expand the capacity of NHS patients to act as real consumers and it may be the case that the private medical sector allows people to make more informed choices about the care they receive. We shall explore whether this is in fact the case in subsequent chapters and for the moment continue to use the term 'consumer' in inverted commas.

What of the possible explanations for the apparent increase in 'consumer' demand for private medical insurance and private medical care (Laing, 1985)? One of the most common is the claim that there has been an increase in dissatisfaction with the NHS. For example, according to Bosanquet (1988), 39 per cent of those surveyed in the *Social Attitudes Survey* in 1987 were generally dissatisfied with the NHS, compared with 25 per cent in 1983. There was discontent about waiting lists, inadequate staffing levels and day-to-day organization of hospital services, although there was confidence in the overall quality of NHS care and health was seen as a priority for Government spending.

There are, at least, three possible reasons for this apparent increase in dissatisfaction. First it may be a response to the perceived deterioration in the service stemming from constraints on public expenditure and concessions to the private sector. Alternatively, it may be a product of the vehemence with which the view that the NHS is collapsing has been expressed in public debates over the last few years. For example, as Day and Klein (1989) suggest, while the medical profession has regularly pointed to the shortcomings of the service as a way of drumming up support for extra funding throughout the history of the NHS, the public debate in the 1980s was specifically characterized by the ferocity of the confrontation between the profession and the Government.

The third explanation suggests that mounting dissatisfaction with the NHS may be associated with broader social changes in the social relations of consumption. For Saunders (1989), the increase in disposable incomes amongst middle-class and working-class households has created the conditions which have led to a widespread desire for personal control in the sphere of consumption. On this argument the dissatisfaction may be a response to increasing consumer expectations about the choice and standard of service in the light of higher disposable income and not merely a response to the perceived decline in its quality. Certainly, for those who can afford it, as Horne (1986) shows, the perceived attractions of the private sector are usually articulated in terms of choice, privacy and control such as choice of consultant, pre-arranged admission or having a private room.

However, improved material circumstances may not be the only explanation for these changing expectations. As we have already argued, the last decade has seen the emergence of neo-liberalism as an ideological force, emphasizing personal control, self-reliance and individual responsibility. It may be that insofar as the growth of private health insurance reflects changing expectations, these stem from an acceptance of neo-liberal values and a belief that private health insurance enhances control over health and its management.

Whether or not this is so remains an open question and reveals how little we actually know about why people decide to subscribe to private health insurance and why they use it. It is these questions which we shall be focusing on in the following chapters.


## INTRODUCING THE STUDY

In order to understand people's involvement with private health insurance it is necessary to understand how they evaluate the adequacy of health care in general. As was shown previously, some of the debate about the growth of private health insurance and the expansion of private acute medical care has been couched in terms of increasing dissatisfaction with specific areas of the NHS. For example, Taylor-Gooby (1986) concluded on the basis of the survey data he had collected, that despite apparent dissatisfaction with the NHS the majority of people felt that provision of both publicly and privately financed health care were not incompatible and favoured the provision of both forms.

While such surveys have value in their own right they do have serious limitations. In particular, while they provide the basis for constructing patterns of association between attitudinal variables, they tell us little about why these relationships exist or about the logic of reasoning that is used. Evidence from small-scale sociological studies (Calnan, 1988; Calnan and Williams, 1992) has shown that patients have their own rationale for evaluating health care which is shaped by elements associated with the context of their daily lives. Contrary to evidence found in survey research into patient satisfaction, these studies have shown that patients have clear criteria both for evaluating medical procedures and for judging the abilities of their family doctors. This suggests that a qualitative methodology might be more fruitful in explaining why people decide to subscribe to private health insurance and use it and how they evaluate private and NHS services. Such an approach shifts attention away from explaining action in terms of medical rationality towards attempting to understand lay people's actions in terms of their own logic, knowledge and beliefs which in turn are closely tied to the social context and circumstances in which these people carry out their daily activities (Dingwall, 1976). The image of the lay person is of one who is active and critical, who has a complex system of theories about illness and medicine, who manages his or her own health requirements and who is discriminating in the use of knowledge, advice and expertise. This does not just represent a theoretical perspective of those who advocate a micro-sociological approach, but is derived from empirical studies of illness behaviour (Calnan, 1987) which have shown that people have more control over their illness than is sometimes thought and have 'good' reasons for deciding to seek professional help.

The adoption of a qualitative methodology which aims both to examine the meaning and rules that people use to make decisions and evaluate health care and to examine the circumstances in which these decisions are made implies that it would be inappropriate to pre-define the concepts and specific questions that need to be examined. However, we take the view that qualitative research, like other forms of research, is necessarily informed by current theoretical ideas and that the research process involves their development and refinement (Geertz, 1973; Rose, 1982; Hammersley, 1985). We thus believe it is important to clarify at this stage the theoretical framework which we have employed and the way in which it shaped the focus of the study.

Qualitative research into patterns of illness behaviour and patient satisfaction indicate that decisions to use private health care and lay evaluation of health care may be influenced by the level and nature of the individual's (and his or her close friends' and relatives') experiences of health care and by the specific reasons why the sufferer or his/her family sought medical care in a specific instance. The latter element is well illustrated by a study (Calnan, 1983) which examined patients' decisions to go to a hospital accident and emergency department as opposed to a general practitioner. From the provider's point of view there was an element of choice for the patient. For the patient this notion of choice was not particularly appropriate as decisions about where to seek medical care were clear-cut once the problem was identified. The hospital accident and emergency department was seen as the setting for instrumental care and thus was evaluated in terms of speed, convenience and medical care. General practice, on the other hand, was seen as a setting for complaints where there was uncertainty about what was wrong, and general practitioners were evaluated in terms of their communication skills and the time they gave to the patient. Thus, patients may have context-specific demands when they seek professional medical help and evaluate their experiences of health service provision accordingly.

In addition to individuals' and their significant others' past experience of health care and the context-specific reasons for seeking help, there are also other more general elements at the macro-level which might shape lay perceptions and decision-making. Of these the socio-political values or ideology upon which the particular health-care system is based is perhaps the most important as it structures in a general way how people perceive health care, how they should use it and what they have to do to get it. Studies examining health care under the NHS quite understandably take for granted the ideological beliefs associated with the system. However, when private health care is being examined, even under a predominantly NHS, it might be important to consider the contrasting values associated with the two systems as they have different implications for the patient. In the previous section it was shown that the NHS was associated with the 'social equity model' of health care. The restricted choice and the idea that providers will define patients' needs appear to have led to an acceptance of the philosophy of the provider. 'Don't waste the doctor's time with trivia,' is an example of this philosophy which has been taken on to some degree by patients (Calnan, 1983).

Professional control and influence over provision and resources is also prevalent in the 'market economy model', primarily because health care has special qualities which differentiate it from other consumer products (Titmuss, 1969). However, in this model there is a greater risk of over provision for those who can pay and lack of access for those who cannot (Hunter, 1983). Moreover, the emphasis in this case is on individual choice, responsibility and consumer sovereignty with providers competing in response to consumer demand.

While the research reported here is concerned with the decision to subscribe to and use private health care it is important to see if so-called 'consumers' have different 'expectations' and 'beliefs' and adopt different patterns of help-seeking behaviour when they use this form of care as opposed to the NHS. In particular, it will be interesting to see if they 'shop around' between the systems, adopting the rational, business model of buying health care under the market economy.

These conceptual issues, then, shaped the theoretical approach adopted in the study and in some ways they shaped the methodology used too. As was argued previously, sociological studies of illness and help-seeking behaviour have clearly shown the value of using qualitative methods to investigate questions about lay decision-making.

Having clarified these issues the next problem we faced was to identify and gain access to a sample of current private health subscribers. The small proportion of the adult population who are covered by private health insurance, the variety of schemes that these policyholders are involved with and the fact that the majority of policyholders are confined to a certain social group in the population led to a two-stage method being adopted. The first stage involved using a postal survey to identify the groups for in-depth investigation; in the second stage, individuals from these groups were interviewed with the aid of a checklist.

The first stage of the project thus consisted of sampling people who have a high likelihood of having private medical insurance, i.e. men aged between 35 and 55 in relatively high income groups. A sample of 3060 men aged between 35 and 55 was selected from the age–sex registers of four general practices based in relatively affluent areas of Kent. The accuracy of these age–sex registers is difficult to estimate and the error rate appears to vary between 10 and 25 per cent (Bowling and Jacobson, 1989). Self-completed questionnaires were sent to each person in the sample. Fifty-five per cent (1688) sent back a completed questionnaire. However, in one practice ($N = 923$), the response rate was particularly low (47 per cent), in part perhaps because of the absence of an age–sex register. Included in the questionnaire were details about whether the person was currently subscribing to private health insurance and the use made of it; his socio-political beliefs about the health service and

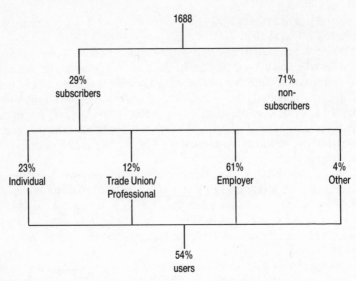

**Figure 1**   Distribution of 1688 completed questionnaires

satisfaction with patterns of use of the health services; his health status (measured by *General Household Survey* questions about perceived health status) and socio-demographic characteristics; and a question asking if she would take part in the second stage.

Twenty-nine per cent (485) of the respondents to the postal questionnaire reported that they were current subscribers and Figure 1 shows the distribution of type of scheme to which the subscribers belonged. The method of paying for insurance can take a number of forms within employer and trade union cover: that is, the subscribers may pay all of the costs, part or none (usually at least the payment of the tax cost is undertaken by the subscriber). Thus, in terms of mode of payment, subscribers could be categorized as individual subscribers (38 per cent), company subscribers (employer pays all, 35 per cent), joint (employer and employee share the costs, 23 per cent) and other (4 per cent).

The second stage of the study involved tape-recorded interviews (54 per cent of the total were willing to be interviewed) with small random samples of men who were stratified into one of the following three groups according to whether they had:

(i)    personally chosen to take out private health insurance
(ii)   been co-opted into employer-run schemes
(iii)  chosen not to subscribe to a scheme.

Sixty interviews lasting about two hours each were conducted with individuals from these three groups (distributed equally between the groups on a quota basis) in 1989 and the early months of 1990. The interview guide was organized around themes directly related to the research questions, and from issues which emerged in 20 pilot interviews at a company which had blanket private health insurance cover for their employees. Using a series of prompts, individuals were asked first about their health status and patterns of help-seeking behaviour. With reference to private health insurance respondents were asked about current and past enrolment in private health insurance schemes, knowledge about the extent of coverage, the decision-making associated with their subscription and its use, and finally the pathway taken to private health care and how the pattern of use fitted in with the use of the NHS. All respondents were also asked about their perceptions of the private and public provision of a range of other welfare services.

In the following chapters we analyse the data from these interviews, along with some of the questionnaire results, in terms of these themes. Thus in Chapter 2 we begin to explore why some people decide to subscribe to private health insurance given that similar services to those available privately are provided free of charge on the NHS. This will involve reviewing the available survey evidence from our local study in Kent and from other sources which portray the national picture. The aim will be to try to identify the typical subscriber, not just in terms of their personal characteristics but also their political values, and to see whether dissatisfaction with the NHS is a major reason for taking out private health cover.

In Chapter 3 we try to develop our analysis of the motives for subscribing with the aid of our interview data. We shall show that the survey results which suggest that dissatisfaction with the NHS is a major reason for subscribing to private health insurance is misleading and that such dissatisfaction does not necessarily impact on broad principles about the organization and funding of health care as a whole.

In Chapter 4 we shift our focus to why people decide to use their insurance. This is important because there is evidence that a considerable proportion of subscribers do not actually do so and some stop paying as a result. The evidence from our study is that only about half of the subscribers actually use their insurance and that the decision to do so is often influenced by concern about resources such as time and money.

In Chapter 5 we look at the broader issue of the social meaning of private health insurance and its use and the extent to which those who satisfy their need for health care through the private sector manifest different political values and cultural perceptions from those who continue to rely on the state for medical treatment. This will enable us to comment on whether the debate about social divisions in UK society are more usefully explored by concentrating on divisions within the sphere of consumption rather than production. These arguments and those of the previous chapters will be summarized in Chapter 6, before drawing out the sociological and policy implications of our study.

# 2

# A TYPICAL PRIVATE HEALTH INSURANCE SUBSCRIBER

As stated in Chapter 1, one of our major aims is to try to explain why some people decide to subscribe to private health and why they use it given that similar services are provided free of charge by the NHS. In this chapter we begin to explore the first of these questions by examining the available survey and interview data from a local study in Kent and other survey data which portray the national picture. The intention is to see if it is possible to identify the 'typical' subscriber, not just in terms of their personal characteristics, but also in terms of their political values and attitudes to the health service and the Welfare State. This should shed some light on the value of some of the speculative explanations for consumer-led growth in private health insurance which were outlined in Chapter 1. One of the most commonly suggested is that people opt for private health insurance because they are dissatisfied with the NHS or certain aspects of it. However, before these explanations are assessed it is important to present briefly some details about the subscribers and the nature of their insurance cover.

## THE SUBSCRIBERS

Twenty-nine per cent of the sample of 1688 middle-aged men (aged 35–55 years) reported that they were currently subscribing to some kind of private health insurance scheme and a further 8 per cent said they used to subscribe but that their subscription had lapsed. Also, one respondent said he had attempted to join a private health insurance scheme but had not been accepted.

The vast majority (61 per cent) of subscribers were in company schemes run by employers, another 12 per cent were in group

schemes organized by a trade union or professional association
and 23 per cent were in individual schemes. The pattern of payment for the subscription was slightly different in that in some
company schemes both the employer and the employee made a
contribution. Thus 38 per cent of the subscribers paid for the
entire subscription, another 35 per cent had their subscription paid
entirely by the employer and the remainder contributed jointly.

The extent of coverage also varied. The most common form of
coverage included both the subscriber and his family (60 per cent)
and a further 20 per cent had insurance cover which covered the
subscriber and his partner. Only 12 per cent had a policy which
covered themselves alone. Subscribers were also asked about the
extent of their policy cover and whether it excluded payment for
private medical treatment for certain medical conditions. Thirty-
four per cent reported that their policy excluded payments
specifically for psychiatric problems, pregnancy, dental and eye
treatment, cosmetic surgery, addiction, alternative medicine,
sterilization, AIDS and treatment required as a result of war or
civil disobedience. A further 39 per cent said that their policy did
not have any exclusions and a further 23 per cent admitted that
they did not know the extent of their coverage. Certainly, from the
interviews which we undertook, we gained the impression that
there was considerable uncertainty about the extent of care or the
restrictions on claims allowed in their policy. However, if they did
know, it was never a definite answer but rather prefixed with 'I
think':

> 'I think I can have anything done, the wife cannot. I do know
> that she's not covered for anything she's ever wanted doing. It
> happened a lot at work, people starting using the scheme and
> then found they were not covered.'

This uncertainty, as the previous extract implies, was particularly the case with company subscribers who were less likely to be
clear about their entitlements:

> 'I'm not clear on the limits. It's imagined to be limitless, but
> there must be a limit on it. I actually went to the personnel
> department this morning because I thought you might ask this
> question, to try and find out and the girl said, "There is no
> simple rule, there's different conditions covered by different

amounts". So I can't tell you we were never told but I know people have got their limits.'

Thus, a number of company subscribers talked of going over their limit or knowing colleagues where this had happened:

'I went over the limit, but the consultant fiddled it to look like separate operations.'

The individual subscribers, as might be expected, appeared to be more knowledgeable and generally stated that there were no exclusions. Others said that the only exclusion was either with existing conditions or limitations on the cost of treatment.

'Covers me for everything, except what I had last week, which was an ongoing condition . . . I was cross I wasn't covered. I should imagine there are more exclusions if I read the small print.'

'No, I don't think there are any exclusions. To be quite honest, I haven't read every word that is in the prospectus but, as far as I know, it covers you for everything. I don't think there are any limits.'

However, there were a minority of subscribers who were very knowledgeable. For example, all those subscribing to a 'cheaper' hospital plan were aware of the 'six-week clause' which restricted use of the private sector to when the NHS waiting list was longer than six weeks, and some could quote the extent of financial coverage:

'I get £8000 a year cover for my family.'

The most informed people were those, not surprisingly, who needed to be. It is well known that those with chronic illness or disability and their representatives become well informed about medical matters during the course or development of the illness. However, we found that this extends to knowledge of private health insurance. For example, a respondent whose son had a brain tumour had worked out exactly for which operations and treatments he could use his insurance.

In addition to confusions and uncertainties over entitlements, the interviews also revealed an ambiguity over the definition of what constitutes private health insurance coverage. Twenty-nine per cent of the respondents in the postal survey reported that they were subscribers to private health insurance yet the random interviews revealed a small number in schemes such as the Hospital Savings Association (HSA) where subscription costs are negligible.

'I ticked "yes" on the form (postal questionnaire) but the HSA is not like BUPA or PPP. We don't pay very much, but we do get benefits . . . I get £40 a day when I'm in hospital and a third off for dental treatment.'

While these schemes are not new and are subscribed to by a minority, including them in the same category as the more comprehensive schemes in survey results may lead to an overestimate of the level of insurance cover, particularly in an ideological climate where insurance is viewed positively.

## THE TYPICAL SUBSCRIBER?

According to the data of the *General Household Survey* (see Chapter 1), the typical subscriber to private health insurance is a middle-aged man with a professional or managerial occupation living in the South East of England. Hence, we targeted this particular group for investigation. However, our study also threw some light on some other characteristics. First, in terms of economic activity, subscribers were more likely to be employees than self-employed and more likely to come from Registrar General Social Classes I and II than their counterparts who were non-subscribers. Second, there was no evidence to show that health status as perceived by the respondent was any better or worse than for the non-subscribers in the sample. However, this must be interpreted with a degree of caution given that the population from which the sample was taken was skewed towards the affluent middle class. Third, and perhaps not surprisingly, subscribers were more likely to say they intended to vote Conservative (65 per cent) in the next General Election compared with the non-subscribers (50 per cent) who were more likely to say they would vote Labour. However, the support for the Labour party in the sample as a whole was low.

The high proportion of subscribers who were Conservative party supporters might reflect a certain set of political values – a possibility which will be explored later in this chapter. First, however, it is important to see whether subscribers differed from non-subscribers in terms of their attitudes to health care and also their use of such care. Before we focus on this specific question it is necessary to look at levels of satisfaction in the sample as a whole and whether these portray a similar picture to those found in the national studies.

The *Social Attitudes Survey* (Taylor-Gooby, 1991b) showed an increase in public dissatisfaction with the NHS between 1983 and 1990. In 1983, only 26 per cent were 'quite' or 'very' dissatisfied with 'the way the NHS is run these days', compared with 39 per cent in 1986 and 47 per cent in 1990. In the local study in 1989, the proportion was much lower with 24 per cent stating that they were dissatisfied. Results from the *Social Attitudes Survey* show that concern about the service has increased equally among all social groups, although it remains less prevalent among Conservative sympathizers, the elderly and working-class people.

Evidence from a comparative analysis (Judge *et al.*, 1992) of results from public opinion surveys suggests that the levels of dissatisfaction reported in the *Social Attitudes Survey*, at least at the general level, may be inflated. For example, in the National Association for Health Authority and Trusts (NAHAT) surveys, while a similar increase in dissatisfaction was found between 1985 and 1988, rising from 10 per cent to 17 per cent, it fell to 12 per cent in 1991. It is clear that these levels of dissatisfaction are much lower than that found in the *Social Attitudes Survey*. Judge and his colleagues (1992) suggest that the reason for this apparent discrepancy is probably due to the difference in context, wording and ordering of the questions in the two surveys. In their view the *Social Attitudes Survey* asks for a more politicized opinion particularly in its question about general levels of satisfaction with the NHS as a whole (Judge *et al.*, p. 894):

> the evidence suggests that the main force making for greater dissatisfaction was increased politicisation rather than changing reactions to the services day by day . . . NHS itself is a political issue, about which many people's views will be influenced by their political attitudes and by the media . . .

The questions in the NAHAT survey on the other hand, while not divorced from other considerations, were more firmly grounded in local knowledge and experiences. There were, however, similarities between the surveys in terms of the gradient in dissatisfaction reported across different aspects of the NHS. In both the national and local surveys the major source of dissatisfaction was with attending hospital as an outpatient, and to a lesser extent, being in hospital as an inpatient. In both these areas there was a marked increase in dissatisfaction between 1983 and 1990. The level of dissatisfaction with the hospital inpatient care was 12 per cent in the local study compared with 15 per cent in the *Social Attitudes Survey* in 1990. However, the reverse pattern was true for hospital out-patient care with 31 per cent saying they were dissatisfied with this aspect in the local study compared with 28 per cent in the 1990 *Social Attitudes Survey* (Taylor-Gooby, 1991b).

Concern about hospital services focused mainly on the hospital waiting list for a non-emergency operation and the waiting time before getting an appointment with a hospital consultant. In the 1990 *Social Attitudes Survey*, 83 per cent and 82 per cent, respect-ively, said these areas were in need of a lot or some improvement. The comparable figures for the local study were 92 per cent and 87 per cent. However, while these areas were major sources of concern at the national level between 1983 and 1990, public anxiety about these and other areas had not risen perceptibly.

Analysis of public opinion data (Judge *et al.*, 1992) also shows that in these studies there is usually a higher level of dissatisfaction found in responses to general questions where respondents are asked to express a value judgement on the running of the NHS, whether nationally or locally, compared with questions about specific services. However, in the local study no such difference was evident. This might be because all the attitudinal questions were asked after a series of questions about health status and previous use of health services. Consequently, the answers would have been grounded in the respondents' previous experiences.

The picture which emerges from the *Social Attitudes Survey* and the local survey is one of general support for the NHS. The vast majority believe that government should have a responsibility for the provision of health care and there has been an increase in those who believe the state should spend more on the health services. It is possible that this evidence of support may be an artefact of the type of questions used, especially given the level of dissatisfaction ex-pressed about the organization of the NHS hospital sector, particu-larly waiting times and waiting lists. However, higher levels of satisfaction have been found with other services such as those provided by general practitioners.

Even so, we shall need to ask whether subscribers are more dissatisfied with the health service than the non-subscribers. The data from the *Social Attitudes Survey* suggest that subscribers are only slightly more dissatisfied with the way in which the NHS runs nowadays. Of those with private health insurance in 1990, 51 per cent said that they were quite or very dissatisfied with the NHS compared with 47 per cent of those without private health insurance. Taylor-Gooby (1991b) threw some light on this relationship by examining the association between levels of satisfaction with the NHS and allegiance to the NHS for the groups with and without private health insurance. He showed that irrespective of whether the respondent subscribed to private health insurance or not, increased levels of dissatisfaction were associated with an increase in allegiance to the NHS. For example, of those who had private health insurance and who reported that they were very dissatisfied with the NHS, 69 per cent said that the Government should increase taxes to pay for extra spending, 71 per cent said that the NHS should be first priority for extra spending and 94 per cent said it was definitely the Government's responsibility to provide health care for the sick. The respective figures for those without private health insurance and who were also very dissatisfied with the NHS for each of these statements was 73 per cent, 64 per cent and 92 per cent. On this basis, Taylor-Gooby (1991b) concluded that those with easiest access to private health care are, in general, as likely to want more state provision as those who do not have easy access to private medicine.

The evidence from this local study shows a slightly different picture. There was a statistical relationship between current subscriptions to private health insurance and levels of satisfaction with the health service or certain parts of it (see Table 1). Those who reported current subscriptions to private health insurance were divided into three groups according to the source of payment. It was felt that this classification provided a better measure of the extent to which the respondent was committed to a scheme than using a classification which simply identified the type of scheme the respondent subscribed to. The 'current' non-subscribers were divided up into those who had 'never' subscribed and those whose subscription had 'lapsed'.

Table 1 shows that there appeared to be a generally lower level of satisfaction with the NHS amongst subscribers than non-subscribers and that these differences were more marked than in those found in the *Social Attitudes Survey*. However, there were also differences between the types of subscriber with those in employer-run schemes

**Table 1**  Satisfaction with NHS and private health insurance*

| Question | Non-subscriber to private health insurance | | Subscriber to private health insurance | | | Total |
| --- | --- | --- | --- | --- | --- | --- |
| | Never (%) | Lapsed (%) | Employer pays (%) | Joint payment (%) | Individual pays (%) | (%) |
| *How satisfied would you say you are with the way in which the National Health Service runs nowadays?* | | | | | | |
| Very satisfied | 12 | 7 | 7 | 2 | 4 | 10 |
| Quite satisfied | 43 | 43 | 31 | 25 | 23 | 38 |
| Neither | 23 | 27 | 28 | 28 | 35 | 26 |
| Quite dissatisfied | 15 | 13 | 24 | 25 | 24 | 17 |
| Very dissatisfied | 5 | 9 | 7 | 19 | 11 | 7 |
| N = | 1047 | 135 | 169 | 130 | 181 | 1688 |
| *How satisfied or dissatisfied are you with the way in which each of these parts of the NHS runs nowadays?* *(i) Attending hospital as an outpatient* | | | | | | |
| Very satisfied | 14 | 9 | 8 | 3 | 4 | 11 |
| Quite satisfied | 32 | 30 | 20 | 16 | 17 | 28 |
| Neither | 14 | 17 | 12 | 17 | 13 | 14 |
| Quite dissatisfied | 15 | 22 | 28 | 28 | 28 | 20 |
| Very dissatisfied | 8 | 10 | 17 | 20 | 14 | 11 |
| Don't know | 12 | 12 | 12 | 15 | 20 | 13 |
| N = | 1047 | 135 | 169 | 130 | 181 | 1688 |

## (ii) Local doctors/GPs

| | | | | | | |
|---|---|---|---|---|---|---|
| Very satisfied | 43 | 37 | 31 | 30 | 35 | 39 |
| Quite satisfied | 43 | 45 | 52 | 45 | 44 | 45 |
| Neither | 8 | 4 | 9 | 12 | 11 | 8 |
| Quite dissatisfied | 4 | 10 | 5 | 11 | 7 | 5 |
| Very dissatisfied | 1 | 2 | 2 | 2 | 2 | 2 |
| Don't know | <1 | 1 | – | – | – | – |
| N = | 1047 | 135 | 169 | 130 | 181 | 1688 |

*Say whether you think the NHS is, on the whole, satisfactory or in need of improvement*

### (i) Hospital waiting list for non-emergency operations

| | | | | | | |
|---|---|---|---|---|---|---|
| In need of a lot of improvement | 56 | 60 | 54 | 62 | 61 | 51 |
| In need of some improvement | 34 | 33 | 36 | 30 | 31 | 36 |
| Satisfactory | 5 | 4 | 7 | 5 | 6 | 9 |
| Very good | 1 | – | – | 1 | 1 | 1 |
| N = | 1047 | 135 | 169 | 130 | 181 | 1688 |

### (ii) Quality of medical treatment in hospital

| | | | | | | |
|---|---|---|---|---|---|---|
| In need of a lot of improvement | 3 | 3 | 2 | 7 | 6 | 4 |
| In need of some improvement | 21 | 24 | 19 | 27 | 27 | 22 |
| Satisfactory | 47 | 46 | 51 | 51 | 54 | 48 |
| Very good | 25 | 22 | 23 | 13 | 12 | 22 |
| N = | 1047 | 135 | 169 | 130 | 181 | 1688 |

* Missing answers are included in the percentages of all Tables, which explains why not all reported percentages added up to 100%

**Table 2** Use of health services and private health insurance

| Use of health services over the last 12 months | Non-subscriber to private health insurance | | Subscriber to private health insurance | | | Total |
| --- | --- | --- | --- | --- | --- | --- |
| | Never (%) | Lapsed (%) | Employer pays (%) | Joint payment (%) | Individual pays (%) | (%) |
| *GP visits* | | | | | | |
| None | 33 | 31 | 31 | 29 | 30 | 32 |
| Once | 24 | 24 | 26 | 30 | 25 | 25 |
| Twice | 17 | 17 | 20 | 15 | 24 | 18 |
| Three times | 8 | 9 | 7 | 4 | 8 | 7 |
| Four times | 6 | 6 | 9 | 10 | 2 | 9 |
| Five times or more | 8 | 10 | 6 | 10 | 8 | 9 |
| Don't know | 1 | 2 | – | 1 | – | 1 |
| N = | 1047 | 135 | 169 | 130 | 181 | 1688 |
| *Outpatient* | | | | | | |
| (i) *NHS hospital* | | | | | | |
| None | 71 | 65 | 84 | 86 | 78 | 10 |
| Once | 11 | 16 | 6 | 6 | 8 | 10 |
| Twice | 5 | 4 | 3 | 2 | 4 | 5 |
| Three times | 4 | 6 | 2 | 2 | 1 | 3 |
| Four times or more | 5 | 5 | 1 | 3 | 4 | 4 |
| N = | 1047 | 135 | 169 | 130 | 181 | 1688 |

**(ii) Private hospital**

| | | | | | | |
|---|---|---|---|---|---|---|
| None | 92 | 90 | 76 | 79 | 76 | 87 |
| Once | 2 | 3 | 14 | 10 | 8 | 5 |
| Twice | 1 | 1 | 5 | 4 | 4 | 2 |
| Three times | <1 | 2 | 1 | 2 | 1 | 1 |
| Four times or more | 1 | 1 | 2 | 2 | 2 | 1 |
| N = | 1047 | 135 | 169 | 130 | 181 | 1688 |

*Admission*

**(i) NHS hospital**

| | | | | | | |
|---|---|---|---|---|---|---|
| None | 88 | 87 | 95 | 97 | 93 | 90 |
| Once | 6 | 7 | 1 | 2 | 1 | 5 |
| Twice | 1 | 2 | 1 | 1 | 1 | 1 |
| Three times or more | 1 | – | – | – | – | 1 |
| Don't know | – | – | – | – | – | – |
| N = | 1047 | 135 | 169 | 130 | 181 | 1688 |

**(ii) Private hospital**

| | | | | | | |
|---|---|---|---|---|---|---|
| None | 96 | 96 | 91 | 94 | 90 | 95 |
| Once | 1 | 1 | 5 | 5 | 3 | 2 |
| Twice or more | – | – | 1 | – | 1 | <1 |
| N = | 1047 | 135 | 169 | 130 | 181 | 1688 |

being more satisfied than those in the other groups. The group which paid for insurance jointly with their employers showed the lowest level of satisfaction. However, it was also apparent that the 'lapsed' subscribers' views were closer to those of 'current subscribers' than to those who never subscribed. Table 1 also shows levels of satisfaction with a range of different types of service. Again a greater level of dissatisfaction was found amongst those with private health insurance and this was evident for outpatient services, waiting lists, non-urgent operations and general practitioner care.

What is the source of this dissatisfaction? Is it based on experience of use of the NHS or is it tied to broader socio-political values? According to evidence presented in Table 2 this dissatisfaction does not appear to be tied to their recent experience of use of NHS hospital outpatient or inpatient services as subscribers have tended, over the previous 12 months, to make less use of these services than non-subscribers.

Perhaps the dissatisfaction amongst subscribers to private health insurance is based on past experience (prior to the last 12 months) of use of NHS hospital care or maybe it is linked to broader socio-political values. As was shown earlier in this chapter, subscribers were more likely to support the Conservative party than non-subscribers. At a broad level, the analysis showed that support for the private sector was more prevalent amongst subscribers; only 3 per cent of those with individual subscriptions, 5 per cent of those in employer-paid schemes and 2 per cent of those where schemes were jointly paid stated that the private sector should be abolished, compared with 9 per cent of the non-subscribers. In contrast, while 28 per cent of non-subscribers thought that private care should be available in the NHS and outside it, 54 per cent of those in employer-paid schemes, 52 per cent in individual-paid schemes and 51 per cent in schemes where there was joint payment thought it should be available in both the public and private sectors.

Socio-political beliefs and values in relation to publicly funded and privately funded health care were explored in more depth through a series of statements with which respondents were asked whether they agreed or disagreed, on a five-point scale. There were two sets of statements. The first focused on general beliefs about health care and examined dimensions such as 'egalitarianism', 'individualism' versus 'collective responsibility', 'consumer- versus provider-defined need' and 'free market economy versus state intervention' (see Table 3). The second set of statements focused on

**Table 3** Socio-political beliefs and private health insurance (PHI)

| Percentage who agree 'strongly' or 'a little' with the following statements | Non-subscriber to private health insurance | | Subscriber to private health insurance | | | Total |
|---|---|---|---|---|---|---|
| | Never (%) | Lapsed (%) | Employer pays (%) | Joint payment (%) | Individual pays (%) | (%) |
| 1 The NHS should only be available to those on low incomes | 11 | 10 | 11 | 5 | 10 | 10 |
| 2 The increasing provision of private health care creates further division between rich and poor | 76 | 76 | 65 | 62 | 58 | 71 |
| 3 Having to pay encourages patients to be more responsible about their health | 46 | 43 | 60 | 58 | 63 | 51 |
| 4 Government-funded health care encourages patients' dependence on the state | 29 | 31 | 33 | 32 | 40 | 32 |
| 5 Government should raise taxes to increase spending on the NHS | 58 | 52 | 45 | 56 | 43 | 55 |
| 6 Governments should make private health insurance tax deductible | 49 | 63 | 70 | 69 | 82 | 58 |
| 7 Private health care is undermining the NHS | 46 | 58 | 24 | 33 | 22 | 43 |
| 8 Health care should be treated like any other commodity where you shop around to get the best buy | 32 | 48 | 54 | 55 | 51 | 39 |
| N = | 1047 | 135 | 169 | 130 | 181 | 1688 |

specific beliefs about the qualities of private health care as against NHS care (see Table 4).

First, in relation to the sample as a whole, only a small minority thought the NHS should be available solely to those on low incomes and almost three-quarters thought that private health care was creating further inequalities. This appears to suggest that there was general support for the egalitarian principles associated with the NHS and concern that these principles might be threatened by private health care. However, the majority did not think that private health care was undermining the NHS, suggesting that there was some support for a mixed economy of health care.

In terms of 'collectivism versus individual responsibility', while there was only minority support for the statement 'Government-funded health care encourages patients' dependence on the state', the majority did agree with 'Having to pay encourages patients to be more responsible about their health'.

This mixed picture was repeated in relation to another aspect – 'free market economy versus state involvement'. The majority of respondents supported an increase in spending on the NHS through an increase in taxes but also supported governments making private health insurance tax deductible. However, there was less support for the view that 'Health care should be treated like any other commodity where you shop around to get the best buy'.

Overall, the picture which emerged from the sample's responses to these statements about socio-political beliefs about publicly and privately funded health care shows support both for public funding and the NHS, for provider-defined care but also for private health care in terms of the encouragement of individual responsibility.

The second cluster of belief items covered issues such as the quality of nursing and medical care in the public and private sectors, hospital facilities, overtreatment and underutilization in private hospitals and private health insurance as a status symbol. As Table 4 shows, there was only minority support for the statements that medical care (both doctors and nursing) was better in private hospitals, although there was majority support for the idea that doctors spent more time with patients and facilities were superior in the private sector. Almost three-quarters of the sample thought that payment for treatment would discourage utilization although only one-third of the sample thought private health care encourages overtreatment. Finally, for a large minority private health insurance was perceived as a status symbol.

**Table 4** Beliefs about private versus NHS care and private health insurance (PHI)

| Percentage who agree 'strongly' or 'a little' with the following statements | Non-subscriber to private health insurance | | Subscriber to private health insurance | | | Total |
|---|---|---|---|---|---|---|
| | Never (%) | Lapsed (%) | Employer pays (%) | Joint payment (%) | Individual pays (%) | (%) |
| 1 Nursing care is better under private than NHS | 42 | 45 | 53 | 68 | 52 | 46 |
| 2 Doctors spend more time with their patients in private health care | 60 | 60 | 67 | 64 | 66 | 62 |
| 3 Facilities in private hospitals are far superior to those in NHS | 57 | 55 | 62 | 66 | 64 | 60 |
| 4 Having to pay for treatment would discourage going to the doctor when you need to | 76 | 76 | 62 | 61 | 64 | 72 |
| 5 Patients are given more treatment than they actually need in private care | 37 | 37 | 19 | 20 | 22 | 32 |
| 6 Doctors will look after your health better when there is money involved | 51 | 39 | 41 | 46 | 39 | 48 |
| 7 Having private health insurance is a status symbol | 53 | 46 | 26 | 27 | 21 | 44 |
| $N =$ | 1047 | 135 | 169 | 130 | 181 | 1688 |

Do private health insurance subscribers have a distinct set of beliefs? Table 3 shows the relationship between these general beliefs and subscription to private health insurance. On *almost all* the belief items, there were differences between the subscribers and non-subscribers and the general picture which emerged suggests that subscribers supported a mixed economy of health care more than non-subscribers and provided more support for the values of individual responsibility and consumer sovereignty than non-subscribers.

The second cluster of belief items covering issues such as the quality of nursing and medical care, hospital facilities, overtreatment and underutilization and private health insurance as a status symbol showed consistent differences between the subscribers and non-subscribers with subscribers, as might be expected, being more likely to see the benefits of private health care compared with non-subscribers. However, the major differences appeared between the groups in terms of the negative aspects of private medicine. The dangers of overtreatment and underutilization were much more likely to be identified by non-subscribers than subscribers (Table 4).

In summary, the evidence suggests that subscribers are different to non-subscribers in terms of their socio-political beliefs and in their beliefs about the specific advantages and disadvantages of private medicine.

The picture which emerges from the survey data is that it is possible to characterize the 'typical' private health insurance subscriber in terms of their beliefs and attitudes towards health care. Simply, subscribers are more likely to be dissatisfied with the NHS and this dissatisfaction seems to be tied to their broader socio-political values which put less emphasis on state intervention and more emphasis on individual responsibility, free market principles and consumer sovereignty. Hence, amongst subscribers there is stronger support for a mixed economy of health care because the benefits of the private sector are more readily appreciated.

The explanation which seems to emerge from this evidence is that people tend to opt for private health insurance mainly because of political and ideological beliefs. However, such data give few clues as to why the statistical relationship exists. The aim of the qualitative analysis, therefore, is to explain the possible relationship between socio-political values, pragmatic reasoning and

action. Subscribers may express dissatisfaction and align themselves to certain political values but does this accurately convey the
logic of the reasoning that is used? Generally, the evidence from the
qualitative analysis about how respondents viewed the NHS and
private medicine appeared to support that from the quantitative
analysis. As far as the NHS was concerned, subscribers (both those
in company-run and individual schemes) were more likely to
express dissatisfaction than non-subscribers although this was
directed at certain aspects of the service, particularly waiting lists,
rather than the idea of the NHS *per se*. None of the respondents
identified differences in the quality of treatment in the NHS but
were concerned about receiving 'speedy' treatment.

> 'You can't go when you want to go. If you can go where you
> want and when you want, nobody would be bothered about
> buying health care.'

> 'For convenience I took out the lowest grade [of insurance]
> because of economics, I only wanted to be able to time it, not
> the luxury of it. It's just bed and fed.'

> 'Just in case something major comes up and there's waiting . . .
> a guy came round and told us about the long waiting for hips
> and what have you.'.

> 'I was getting older and you tend to get more ailments, so I
> thought, as I am the bread winner and the wife can't work [she
> has MS], I thought I had better get covered. With the NHS
> there's sometimes a long waiting list.'

It appeared, also, that many subscribers' judgements were likely to
be based on hearsay rather than actual experience.

> 'I've heard it's a lot better . . . the meals are absolutely
> splendid, you have no limited time for visiting, as you have in
> the NHS hospital.'

Differences between the types of subscriber were less evident,
although individual subscribers who were currently self-employed
tended to emphasize the benefits of private medicine in terms of
convenience and minimal disruption to their business:

> 'No problems with using the NHS, but I am self-employed and
> if I need to have something done, I need to do it when I can fit it

in, not have to wait and then be called at an inconvenient moment.'

'It's speed . . . the comfort of instant treatment, which is very important if you are in business.'

There was also evidence that subscribers who were self-employed were concerned about the time and money lost through unplanned hospitalization.

'I am self-employed and time is money . . . and you get superior treatment and more personal attention.'

'Self-employed – no qualms about using NHS, but need convenience.'

Non-subscribers were characterized by their lack of criticism of the NHS and their use of justifications to explain why they evaluated the service in this way.

'At the moment the NHS covers all my needs and in the main it covers them very well. I have affection for it anyway.'

'I think a lot of people that knock the medical service are just bellyaching for the sake of bellyaching to be honest. It's political.'

When asked about the advantages of private medicine, individual subscribers particularly referred to comfort, privacy and individualized care.

'I saw the attractions of private [medicine] after we took it out. When my wife was in hospital, the children could visit at any time, watch cartoons on the telly.'

'I go privately because I can afford to do so, the service I get is better in that they treat you as an intelligent, human being and spend more time with you. I don't blame the NHS for the short-fall but private gives me a top up, a means of being able to circumvent the short-falls. I want attention but I am not dissatisfied with the NHS.'

And there was also one example of the importance of status.

'By using private health, you meet a better class of person. In the NHS there's no telling who you are going to be sitting next to – for some people that's a bad thing.'

However, once again subscribers suggested that the medical care was no different from a technical point of view.

Non-subscribers also imagined there would be advantages in going private (even if they talked more about the problems).

'I suppose it must be like a first-class hotel. You should get better food and more attentive nursing.'

When it came to discussing dissatisfaction with the private sector the responses supported the quantitative data. Thus non-subscribers expressed more criticisms when talking about the public–private mix.

The company and individual subscribers also recognized problems with private provision. Two company subscribers said:

'They take the easy part of the medical field, the bits where the profit is perhaps higher . . . it's not comprehensive enough.'

'It's expensive and there are certain conditions they are not interested in. It's alright if you have got a minor complaint, if you are in and out of hospital pretty quickly, but a long-term illness, you fall back on the NHS.'

The criticisms were directed at expense and non-comprehensiveness of the service, rather than excess treatment. Individual subscribers complained most frequently about cost.

'It's very expensive, you are limited by how much you pay.'

'It's hellishly expensive, at the end of the day you get what you pay for, which means it's out of the reach of some individuals and you are not covered for everything but you know the NHS is there . . .'

Non-subscribers talked of the expense and profit making side of the private sector, but in addition talked of poorer facilities and unnecessary treatment.

'People have unnecessary cosmetic treatment to get their money's worth . . .'

'You get unnecessary operations, doctors will increasingly put business each other's way.'

'Private gives you greater comfort but not as good medical facilities.'

The non-subscribers also saw most problems with the public–private mix of health delivery.

'Private sector is damaging the NHS. It takes resources away, particularly staff trained at state expense. They should pay the state back; working in both is a disgrace. Further privatization will mean the NHS will become a safety net for the old and poor.'

And further privatization was viewed with caution:

'Further privatization will weaken the NHS and lead to a downgrading of the service.'

Company and individual subscribers were difficult to divide in terms of the degree of support for a mixed economy of health care. The private sector was seen to give choice, to reduce waiting lists, and to provide competition. However, the issue of staff working in both sectors and the possible negative implications for the NHS were identified.

'The private system is a parasite in that it poaches staff, resources and equipment . . . you release more places but still the NHS doctors can't be in two places at once. It's swings and roundabouts.'

In summary, the qualitative data suggest that dissatisfaction with the NHS is more strongly voiced by subscribers than the non-subscribers and that this is in part based on hearsay. Certainly if these data in combination with the survey data are taken at face value, it might be argued that the consensus supporting the NHS is beginning to break up. However, as will be shown in Chapter 3, if these beliefs are placed in the broader context of the respondents' socio-political beliefs about the health service, a different picture emerges.

# 3

# PRINCIPLE AND PRACTICE

The picture which emerged from Chapter 2 was that dissatisfaction with the NHS, or some aspects of it, was the major reason why people subscribe to private health insurance and that this dissatisfaction was tied to socio-political values. This chapter, focusing entirely on the interview data, shows that this is a somewhat misleading picture. It specifically examines why and how respondents decided to take out private health insurance. For the most part it shows a stark contradiction between what they called 'principle' and 'practice' and illustrates how they held a number of apparently conflicting values at the same time.

If we start from the premise that values are logically associated with behaviour, we can assume that the holding of insurance should be related to socio-political values with clear differences between subscribers and non-subscribers and, to a lesser degree, between individual and company subscribers. If this is so what values would subscribers to private health insurance be expected to hold? Certainly, they might expect a recognition of the benefits of private medicine, support for a competitive mixed economy, stress upon self-responsibility and agreement, at least in some degree, with the thinking of the Conservative New Right. The evidence from the quantitative analysis (see Chapter 2) showed that subscribers did hold some of these values, but what of the evidence from the qualitative data? We shall consider the responses of each group of subscribers in turn.

## INDIVIDUAL SUBSCRIBERS

A strong degree of coherence between *principle and practice* might be expected amongst those respondents who have bought private health insurance (PHI) as an individual decision. However, this coherence was not very prevalent. For example, one respondent saw the private sector giving better treatment and less waiting.

'The problems that besiege the NHS mean that it should be abolished and that the health sector would move towards US-style medicine. I think it will improve because it will become more of a competition for one company to get more customers than another company.'

At the same time this subscriber's account of his likely behaviour appeared to contradict his beliefs because he said he preferred to use the NHS for a major operation, unless the waiting time was very long.

'In a sense you feel that you are paying for your national health treatment anyway. So although you are paying privately as well, you feel you want to get some sort of service from the NHS.'

Thus, he said that while he would use the NHS because he was still paying National Insurance contributions, in an ideal world he would want to opt out of this altogether. This was one of the four examples of subscribers who were, in principle, pro-private. Of these, three were individual subscribers.

*Interviewer*:  'Would you like to see a completely private system?'
*Respondent*:  'Well, since I am paying so much into private already, I would, if I was financially better off . . . but if I had got a decent NHS I wouldn't need to. It comes back to that again.'

Thus NHS principles were still expressed and the idea of a wholly private sector seemed to hinge on financial considerations. Another recognized the advantages of a free market.

*Respondent*:  'I think the NHS will eventually be abolished.'
*Interviewer*:  'Will that be a good thing?'
*Respondent*:  'Yes, we will be like America, with competition and that will improve health.'

And another supported private health care in principle but wanted the NHS to continue in practice for others.

'If I could go, I would go for a completely private system. I just feel strongly that way . . . but still have an NHS for those that can't afford it. So I wouldn't opt out of National Insurance.'

The remainder of the respondents articulated clear arguments against the principle of private medicine and voiced pro-NHS sentiments. Their ideal system would be an effectively functioning NHS.

'PHI is a necessary evil. Well, ideally, I am all for having an NHS that works, that I don't have to pay through the nose for and an NHS that I could use. But given the amount of waiting and so on, I think it's a necessary evil. I would like in an ideal world to be on NH.'

They recognized that the NHS has problems but also argued that the present system of health care, the mixed economy, provides a structure with choice. If choice exists you 'play the game' and this 'playing the game' may involve rejecting the choice which you 'ideally/ideologically' prefer.

'. . . if it's available on the NHS one ought to use it, but if you're paying for the thing [private] you might as well use it. Once you've got it you might as well use it really. Get your money back!'

Thus, the structure of health care determines to some extent how the respondents behave, at least according to respondents' accounts of their behaviour. Individuals opt out because of the choices offered to them and the belief that the NHS is being run down. In a sense this suggests increased demand is *state induced*.

For others, availing oneself of the private sector was also motivated by practical considerations of employment status. Thus one self-employed respondent saw particular problems of waiting and needed convenient admission dates to minimize the consequences for his business. He preferred the idea of a state run system and like the majority would be prepared to pay more National Insurance contributions to that end. In practice he would like to use NHS first before resorting to the private sector, but as things stood, recognized that private patients had clear advantages.

'I wouldn't want it, not on me conscience. Perhaps that's the wrong word, but I think it's wrong where you can still pay your money and jump the queue. But, at the same time, if there is any queue jumping to be done, I want to be at the front of the queue, as opposed to being at the back. Terrible aren't I, but I am afraid that is the way the world is!'

Others said they would use their PHI if it was more convenient, but stressed the importance of *not* losing the NHS and believed they should continue to pay National Insurance.

'It's my right and duty as someone who earns more than the average to pay my contribution, for those who can't afford to pay.'

'Perhaps someone would say, "Well this is a good thing, privatize medicine," but all I would say is God forbid that that day comes when we have to privatize the totality of medicine. I am only in it because it has certain things wrong with it, but at least I continue to contribute my bit of income to it.'

It could be that the NHS is a very special service – there is a moral connection, a consensual loyalty. Indeed it will be shown in Chapter 5 that respondents have a high regard for the NHS which is not necessarily replicated in regard to other aspects of state provision.

'I was around almost from when the NHS started. I always regarded it as not one of, but *the* most major social reform that had ever come about. And you know, although we are not talking politically I talk as someone who has never in his life voted socialist, I am not a socialist in voting terms – but there are parts of me that say what came in for the NHS was the greatest thing ever. And unfortunately there has been an erosion of that over the years and it has forced more and more people to go into private medicine.'

In summary, for individual subscribers, using PHI was a matter of maximizing their options given the current structure of health care and the practical considerations stemming from being self-employed. For most, however, such contingencies did not challenge their allegiance to the ideals of an NHS, free at the point of access.


## COMPANY SUBSCRIBERS

Senior managers are presumably in a financial position to afford PHI through an individual subscription, and certainly some did hold individual insurance before the introduction of the company scheme. However, the majority of the sample did not have cover prior to joining such a scheme. A number of reasons were cited and it was clear that many were politically and morally against private medicine. Nonetheless, they participated in the scheme.

So why accept? One explanation is that insurance is a company 'perk', offered as part of the wage negotiation or even just given. Subscription to insurance is, at least according to this version of events, *employer induced*. The contradictions are clearly voiced in the following accounts:

'I didn't take it out before for the reason of principle. We didn't think it was a good thing to do . . . It seemed to us that if all the middle-class people could afford to leave the NHS, that would remove some of the pressure to keep it going and keep it good.'

'It was a company perk. I am basically against the private system. I just ignore it – I would never use it . . . But it's all very well me saying that. If it was an emergency and the wellbeing of my family, I don't know. I am principled but also a realist.'

or

> *Respondent*: 'I must admit it is selfish in a way because I wasn't keen on it in the first place, from the principle point of view, but you know we did it [took company insurance] to protect the children's interests. You put your principles to one side . . .'
>
> *Interviewer*: 'Had you thought about it before the company provided the scheme?'
>
> *Respondent*: 'No. I mean if they hadn't provided the scheme, I doubt if I would have done anything about it, to be honest.'

or

'I had different conversations with people at work you know. What shall we do with our principles on this one? . . . Well, there is another chap who was in exactly the same boat. Not keen on the idea, on the simple premise that if you have got a health service provided for on a national basis, through taxation, then it ought to provide for all eventualities. You shouldn't have to pay to go outside that. I think I would probably go [private] just to get my money's worth.'

Thus, while some saw the subscription to private health insurance as posing a problem for them in terms of their principles, once they had decided to join the scheme, they followed a more pragmatic line of reasoning about its actual use. Getting one's money's worth was one approach adopted. Another was that it was to a degree an 'enforced gift'. For example:

'I mean, taking it out, it was given. That's the difficulty. If it exists and someone gives it to you, you will probably say, oh, I will take it.'

or

'I wanted to object because I don't agree with it, but it was offered to me.'

There appears, then, to be a hierarchy of desired goods. PHI has recognized advantages but it is not always a priority and it is often accepted because it is offered. Respondents made this clear when they discussed what they would do if their company subscription lapsed. Certainly it was not a straightforward decision and involved weighing the costs and benefits of taking out a personal subscription and taking into account whether they had made a contribution in the past. Thus, one respondent who received company insurance without any personal contribution, argued he would almost definitely let his subscription lapse.

*Respondent*:    'If I had the choice, I would prefer to spend the money how I want to spend it.'
*Interviewer*:    'Would you take it out yourself?'
*Respondent*:    'I don't think so, no. I can't really see why I should want to take it out because it is rather like insurance really, you know. You can't take it out as soon as someone is ill, you have really got to take it out at a time before it. They are not going to accept you as a member of a scheme if as soon as you sign the dotted line, you say, oh I want to go into hospital.'

However, respondents who were on discount schemes and so had decided to pay already said they would look at the difference in price.

'I do not see myself stopping insuring myself in the foreseeable future, but it would depend on what the new individual premiums were and then review it from that.'

In addition to evaluating cost, one respondent on a discount scheme said he would take account of health needs and standards of treatment.

'I wouldn't have joined prior to the company scheme and I wouldn't look for it in a new job . . . I think we'd sort of stop and look at what is happening so far . . . So far we've not needed to use it [PHI] and have had good treatment on the NHS.'

Thus, company subscribers said they participated in the scheme despite being against PHI in principle. They saw it as a perk or enforced gift and indicated that they would need to calculate the costs and benefits pragmatically before they took out a personal subscription, if the company scheme ceased.

We also discussed with all respondents why they thought companies offered insurance. Some replied that it was given as a perk or because the company was or wanted to appear caring:

'It's now a standard perk and it makes you think the company cares about you.'

For others it was a means of minimizing disruption to productivity:

'So they can slot me into the . . . private hospital, get me mended and back out again onto the front line.'

Finally it was seen as a response to competitor pressure and part of the wage deal process.

'Keeps workers happy and keeps wage costs down. A way of having a pay rise and means they will get their workers back working quicker.'

## NON-SUBSCRIBERS

It might be expected that the comparison group would contain people who do not see problems with the NHS and so do not feel the need to exercise their right of choice. One might also expect this group to have very strong principles against private health insurance, to reject employer-based schemes *or* the need for insurance and indicate a preference for spending their money in different ways. Do we see these *principles* clearly expressed?

Certainly, in this group, principles and practice were most clearly matched with pro-NHS sentiments and a refusal to use the private sector being commonly voiced:

> 'I rebel against private. The NHS is good enough and I pay enough NI [National Insurance] for it and I should help pay for those who can't afford it. Everyone should get the same standard of service.'

> 'I'm against PHI because of principle. If you are a socialist, then private medicine is a sort of total anathema.'

> 'By taking out private health insurance, you are running down the NHS. We'll end up like America with people ill and unable to afford insurance. People opt out of the NHS because they are forced to with waiting. It shouldn't happen.'

The one exception was a respondent who preferred to pay privately because of waiting lists and his poor health status (a history of heart disease) which meant that insurance contributions were very expensive.

The non-subscribers' responses also give us some insight into how principle and practice can become separated. As the following interview shows, principles can be modified when individuals' circumstances intervene.

> *Respondent*: 'I disagree with the principle of private medicine. It damages the NHS and their staff are trained at the expense of NHS – they work both sectors which is a disgrace. But my views are more likely to go towards private as I get older and the possibility of me needing care becomes statistically greater.'
>
> *Interviewer*: 'So principles go in certain circumstances?'
>
> *Respondent*: 'Sure, I have let them get in the way of practicalities, if my principles get incovenient, I have got others! I'm totally against the idea of private medicine in principle but when it comes down to practice and making sure my family is okay, then I will pay. So now I am contemplating a scheme that I don't want to. My political principles say it

> is bad but being self-employed I think about it
> and I could afford it. At the moment principles
> outweigh it, I've looked at it for twenty years and
> still haven't taken it out.'

There were six non-subscribers whose reasoning worked the other way; that is they would have liked to have private health insurance in principle but pragmatic considerations intervened.

> *Interviewer*: 'What stops you joining?'
> *Respondent*: 'Probably three things. The first one, probably,
> is that it would cost me a lot of money. The
> second is that I don't believe it is a full system,
> they will work on certain areas and not on others.
> The third thing is that I am not sure what I feel
> about it politically, how it undermines the
> system. I am one of the very odd people who
> likes the idea of private beds in hospitals because
> the money goes to help pay for National Health
> patients and the consultants who are in the same
> building.'

In this case, principles and the issues of cost are important. Practical considerations also proved more influential for others.

> 'It's going to cost a fortune and doesn't cover you for every-
> thing.'

or

> 'I don't see the need. People that do base their decision to do so
> on conjecture. The impression that treatment is better and
> quicker, if you can believe what you see on TV adverts and that
> sort of thing. If I was wealthy maybe I would take it out as an
> added insurance.'

> 'I am happy with the service . . . I am not against private
> medicine but I am healthy and satisfied.'

## OPTING OUT OF THE NHS?

Finally, the extent of commitment to the NHS was explored by first discussing with all the respondents whether they would pay more for the NHS; or alternatively, whether they would opt out of

National Insurance contributions and move to an entirely private scheme. In a sense this latter possibility was raised to ascertain whether attachment to the NHS was at least in part because of statutory financial commitment. When asked whether they would pay more, all the non-subscribers said they would be willing to do so and one also welcomed minimal charges for certain services on top which he saw as ensuring individual responsibility for health. The remainder accepted the idea of increased expenditure, as the following illustrates:

> 'I would just as soon pay more tax and get an NHS that provided everything that we are likely to need within reason. It would be preferable to change the money and pay insurance to the NHS. If you earn more you should pay more for it.'

Finally, the individual subscribers again said they would be willing to contribute more.

> 'Absolutely, no equivocation on that whatsoever. I would be quite happy to pay more to achieve, first of all two things. One, to achieve social justice for everyone and, secondly, to improve the quality of health medicine.'

> 'Don't privatize further. I would rather see people who can afford it pay more towards NHS.'

The commitment to paying more sometimes contained the proviso that there would be an assurance that the money went to the health service. One individual said:

> 'I don't know where the taxes go. I would love it if they took it from guns and put it into health. If they said they can't do that and said "Will you pay £1 per week more and this will go specifically to the health service?" I would say yes.'

No one said they would not pay extra although one individual subscriber suggested extra payment should be at point of service.

> 'Rather than increase taxes, those who can afford it should pay something when they go. It would perhaps stop people wasting the doctor's time.'

A similar picture was conveyed in response to opting out. Only five respondents said they would welcome this choice; the remainder saw clear disadvantages.

'No because I believe if you start on that particular activity, then all that happens is a worsening of the service provided for other people. If I don't pay my NI, then there would be a lot like me all over the country who would do the same. And if the reduction of that investment in the NHS meant the service would reduce, this may tempt more people to move out . . . I should continue to contribute . . . No. I think I should pay towards the NHS, no, no, no . . .'

The majority then, did not want to opt out of National Insurance contributions even if they were subscribers to private health insurance. There was a recognition that they still used the NHS as a commitment to ensuring that the NHS remained for those on lower incomes.

'No, I'll pay National Health and avail myself of the services of that system, I'm in support of the NHS and will pay for it and would like to see it improve.'

Others justified their views on ideological grounds; a respondent receiving company insurance said:

'I'm against it, I want to see the private sector run down, not expanded. I think it is important that everybody in this country gets the same level of health not just those that can afford it.'

or

'No, I think it is totally wrong. I would fight tooth and nail for the taxes that support the NHS . . . I don't mind if people have extra but they should not be allowed to get out of taxes. Taxes are a part of belonging to a community. You can't un-belong to a community just because you have extra money and buy yourself luxuries.'

'I don't like paying twice, but if I stopped paying the National Health would become even more deflated, so I pay it.'

'It would be nice to opt out, but then the standard would drop in the NHS – it was our choice to pay the extra . . . and I wouldn't want a system like America.'

Indeed, a strongly voiced fear was a development of an America-like system. A respondent receiving company insurance said:

'No I don't want a system like America. I've lived there and doctors are purely financially motivated.'

Interestingly, this illustrates that respondents are committed to the NHS not only on ideological grounds, but also because of practical reasoning, i.e. they need the NHS, particularly for primary care and emergencies. This is apparent in other studies (Busfield, 1990) which show that respondents are aware of the limitations of private health insurance and recognize that they need the NHS to supplement the cover. Furthermore, material/financial considerations mean that they have an interest in maintaining the NHS, as high use of their private facilities inflates private health insurance premiums.

Five of the respondents (three individual, one company, one non-subscriber) said they would like to be able to opt out, if opting out was financially favourable.

'If I could opt out completely, then I would because I feel I could get a pretty good policy with the money I pay into the NHS, although I would sooner the Government sink all the cash into the NHS, so you didn't have to contemplate it.'

'Yes I would be mildly pleased if there was a tax concession. If that came about an awful lot more people would go for it and that will leave more for the people that can't afford it.'

So, again, the more favourable alternative was to commit more resources to the NHS.

'I'd opt out of it, if it didn't cost me any more . . . but I would pay more for the NHS, as long as it's not as outstanding as this poll tax.'

'I'd like to opt out or pay more tax and then I wouldn't have to pay into a private scheme.'

The focus of this chapter has been to examine why people take out private health insurance and in particular whether it is dissatisfaction with the NHS and/or changing values about health and welfare which have a major influence on the decision-making process. The quantitative analysis and the qualitative analysis in Chapter 2 suggest a relationship between subscription and level of satisfaction. It showed that levels of satisfaction were related to mode of payment, with subscribers who paid jointly with their employer being the most dissatisfied. The quantitative analysis also suggested that subscribers to private health insurance did not seem to base their judgements about the health service on recent, personal experience as Saunders and Harris (1989) argued was the case with housing, but on broader ideological values (Taylor-Gooby, 1986). However, one limitation of the quantitative analysis was that it could not account for why the relationship between satisfaction and mode of payment exists, nor show how different aspects of individuals' beliefs are related to each other. The qualitative analysis identified this most clearly by showing how dissatisfaction with aspects of the NHS does not necessarily impact on broad principles about the organization and funding of health care as a whole. The respondents' accounts suggest a strong regard for the NHS and a desire to see a continued service relieved of its present problems. The response to the question of opting out and paying more National Insurance supported this.

Our data certainly suggest that those respondents who are totally pro-private are in a minority. The majority recognize the advantages of private medicine but at the same time exhibit continued support for the Welfare State. Several authors have found similar 'ambivalent' attitudes in their research but have put forward different explanations. For Taylor-Gooby (1987), support for both public and private sectors is explained by self-interest. People derive their rather narrow and individualistic perceptions of interests, according to Taylor-Gooby (1987), from capitalist ideology. Under capitalism, goods and services become private property, so that what are really social relations (e.g. production and consumption of health care) become experienced as exchange relations. Attention is focused on the exchange of things as 'values'. The individual purchase of a good is continually legitimated as the normal way to conduct social relations and self-interest is to do with the capacity to command goods. Thus, there is an in-built prejudice in favour of private provision because it is a market relation. At the same time, the principle of maximizing command over goods produces an interest in favour of the use of state collective services, where these offer a good deal. Thus, there is support for the state service because it is beneficial, but also an endorsement of the legitimacy of the market since this is the basis of consumption in our society. Exit from state use and support for the private sector depends on the balance of state and private provision. The lack of subsidies to the private sector, however, limits enrolment and yet the nature of capitalism ensures support for market principles and privatization. Therefore, self-interest ensures support for both the state and the market and a belief that the private sector offers better facilities is not in opposition to support for state services.

Saunders and Harris (1989), in contrast, interpret ambivalence in a different way. Their empirical findings also show that the majority of their sample is 'ambivalent' although there was evidence of a group of resolute anti-statists. However, this is interpreted as the direct consequence of a state which depends on contributions and as such coerces the public as clients of the state system of health care. As it is impossible to avoid the state sector we are 'trapped consumers'; thus ambivalence is not surprising. Individuals have to pay taxes and want a good service but cannot afford to pay twice. It is therefore logical for them to support state-financed welfare and show preparedness to pay extra for such facilities. Thus, people are pragmatists and support the state but this should not be translated as a popular support. The reason for ambivalence is the lack of choice offered by the state, not the choice offered by the market as Taylor-Gooby would argue.

A further and more materialist explanation of ambivalence emerges from Busfield's (1990) work. She argues that, as has been described previously, support for both sectors emerges because individuals consume both. Typically, the coverage of elective surgery but omission of primary and chronic care from an insurance policy, means that the insured necessarily have to use the NHS which in turn means strong public support for the service. Thus, this approach also incorporates the notion of self-interest, recognizing the material gains from adherence to the NHS.

Our understanding of ambivalence is somewhat different. The majority of our respondents have a strong commitment to the NHS in principle and yet some take out private health insurance. The purchase of private health insurance is not because of a commitment to the market and support for the NHS is not because of the lack of choice. Rather, the very fact that the market provides an alternative (and in 50 per cent of the cases this is an alternative given by companies) which offers some benefits, means that there is support for the private sector. Where Busfield (1990) rightly notes support for the state is dependent on practical need for the continued use of the NHS, we have shown that pragmatic reasoning also intervenes when individuals require the speed or prefer the comfort of private provision. Saunders (1989) argues that respondents do not want to pay twice because they cannot afford it and are constrained to opt for the state sector. We would argue that they do not want to pay twice because the general principle held is pro-NHS.

The NHS is held in high regard even by those who choose to purchase private health insurance. The decision to take out private health insurance, judging from the analysis of the qualitative data, seems to be influenced by a number of different factors. Two of these appear to be related to the supply side, where the employer gives private health insurance as a 'perk' and where the movement towards a mixed economy of health care provides a setting which people 'use' because it is there, not because they prefer such a system. Another three factors are related to the 'demand' side. One of these is associated with the social relations of care in that one of the perceived advantages of private health care is that the patient is treated as an individual. In addition, for some, private health insurance might also be seen as a status symbol. Another is concerned with resource or financial judgements about the loss of time and money associated with waiting lists, or the escalating premiums and increased cost of private health insurance. The third influence is associated with the individual's or families' perceived risk of a deterioration in health status which may lead to a consideration of the advantages and disadvantages of private medicine.

The implications of these findings will be discussed in Chapter 6 but what is of interest also is what use people make of private health insurance once they have chosen to subscribe to it or been 'given' it by their employer. This will be the focus of Chapter 4.

# 4

# THE USE OF PRIVATE HEALTH INSURANCE

In Chapter 3 we focused on decisions to take out private health insurance (PHI). In this chapter we consider why people decide to use their insurance. This is important because although the vast majority of private health-care users are now covered by private health insurance, there is evidence that a considerable proportion of such subscribers do not use their insurance, and others stop paying as a result (Higgins, 1988). We therefore aim to throw some light on the processes involved in deciding to use PHI.

## PATTERNS OF USE

The evidence in this study confirms what was found previously, namely that only about half of subscribers actually used their insurance. On this occasion 54 per cent of subscribers had actually used their insurance and women (66 per cent) were more likely to be users rather than men (51 per cent) and children (35 per cent). There was little variation in use either by age or by health status. In terms of mode of payment the most likely user of insurance was where payment was made jointly (62 per cent). Those in employment-paid schemes (57 per cent) and individual subscribers (55 per cent) used their insurance less. But the least frequent users were the lapsed subscribers (8 per cent of the whole sample) as only 33 per cent had used it. Answers to a self-completed question 'Why are you no longer enrolled?' showed 'low use' to figure as an important influence, along with the expense, change of job or dissatisfaction with the lack of comprehensiveness of the scheme. In each of the main groups of subscribers, most patients were likely to use their insurance for consultation with a specialist, followed by admittance to hospital for surgery.

The quantitative data also provided the basis for identifying patterns of health service utilization. Of particular interest was whether there was any evidence of shopping around between the public and private sectors. The data collected were restricted to use of health services over the past 12 months, and this analysis focuses on hospital outpatient and inpatient service. Our results suggest that there was some, albeit limited, evidence of shopping around. Nine per cent of the sample of middle-aged men reported that in the last 12 months they had used private hospital services (outpatient or inpatient) but only one-third of these reported use of both the public and private sectors. A similar pattern was found for their partners, although the overall utilization rate was slightly higher. Hospital outpatient services provided the setting in which patients most frequently used both public and private sectors. One interpretation of this evidence is that patients tend to stick to using either one sector or the other which suggests that in behavioural terms they establish a consistent pattern of help-seeking behaviour. However, to explain these patterns it is necessary to refer to the data from the qualitative interviews.

## LAY DECISION-MAKING AND USE

The quantitative data tell us little about the rationale behind respondents' pattern of use. Do subscribers automatically consult privately or is their decision-making more calculated? We know that approximately only one-half of subscribers have used their insurance, and that health status is not an adequate explanation for this pattern. Clearly respondents must draw upon certain criteria to decide which type of medical care to utilize. Who and what influences this process? Do some respondents use their insurance more sparingly than others, and why? – the qualitative interviews explored these themes in detail. The conversation ranged over a number of issues relating to use such as why they went privately, who influenced the decision, would they accept contrary advice from an 'expert' (GP/specialist), would they always want to go privately and if not, which NHS service would they envisage using.

First, had our respondents used the private sector? The choice of interviewees was random and produced a cross-section, including non-subscribers who had themselves paid to go privately and subscribers who had either used or not used their insurance. After having ascertained whether respondents had utilized the private sector the next theme explored was 'Why private on this occasion?' Informants' comments gave important insights into the different ways in which private health insurance and the private sector are perceived, as well as the criteria used in making decisions about help-seeking behaviour.

In respect of the decision-making process, six areas appeared pertinent, although in many cases these were not mutually exclusive:

1  Waiting lists
2  Financial criteria
3  The role of others, particularly the GP
4  The designation of medical conditions as public or private
5  The perceived benefits of the private sector and problems associated with the NHS
6  Principles held by respondents.

*Waiting lists*

First, the private sector was utilized because of waiting lists in the NHS which affected the respondents in a number of ways. Some had themselves, or through their GP, ascertained that the waiting period in the NHS was extensive, making the private sector, to some extent, a second option. This was certainly the case for those subscribers covered by the Private Patients Plan, 'Hospital Plan', where one can only go privately if waiting on the NHS is longer than six weeks.

> 'The PPP scheme is where if you can't get into the NHS in six weeks they accept you into the private scheme . . . I didn't go privately, simply because the GP advised me not to. He said, "It won't make any difference, you won't get in any quicker".'

> 'I went privately when I saw the waiting period was nine months. It never really occurred to me to seek private treatment directly.'

However, the length of waiting lists was often not actually investigated. Rather it was assumed to be extensive and private consultations were sought as a result.

> 'It wouldn't occur to me to try the NHS because I should think there would be a waiting list.'

In addition, the private sector is also used to circumvent NHS waiting lists. Many respondents talked of jumping the initial queue by going to see a specialist privately and then going back to the NHS. This clearly benefits non-subscribers who had themselves paid and individual subscribers who have to bear the cost of escalating premiums.

> *Respondent*: 'The only way I'm going to go private is to pay out of my own pocket and use it when I need to do, in order to jump the queue. Basically, last time we did this we paid privately for the wife when she went in for her sterilization. Because we were told by our doctor that if she went through the normal procedures on the NH it might be two or three years, because it was a non-urgent operation. She said, "If you pay private you don't have to pay for the whole thing, you just pay for the consultation and then you jump the queue, because they [NHS] stick you on".'
>
> *Interviewer*: 'So you paid for a private consultation and then went NHS?'
>
> *Respondent*: 'Yes and we were in within three months, so we abused the system. I suppose it's called relaxing your scruples or putting your morals on one side.'

Examples of using the NHS for a consultation and then the private sector for necessary hospitalization were not frequent. Company and joint subscribers more frequently used private inpatient care which may partly be explained by the fact that they do not individually take responsibility for increased premiums if the private sector is used for such hospitalization.

In summary, waiting lists, whether a reality or a perceived problem, play an important role in the use of private health insurance determining the choice of care. Significantly, the waiting list issue is often linked with financial reasoning and this will be illustrated more fully in the following section.

## *Financial criteria*

Financial criteria influence use as respondents may use the private sector to get their money's worth or sometimes use the NHS to keep premiums down. The former criterion was specific to company subscribers who have received PHI as part of a wage deal or company perk. The interplay of finance and waiting appeared a particularly strong influence in terms of saving money and in the circumventing of queues through a private consultation. For example, respondents talked of checking out NHS waiting lists not because the NHS was preferred but for financial reasons – if the waiting is short in the NHS, use this sector and keep the premiums down.

> 'I exploit the NHS first and then if need be use the private. I would use the NHS for hospitalization. You feel if you use it [private] you're going to push up the premiums, so you want to keep it as an insurance, as a back-up. Use it if you can't get satisfaction somewhere else.'

These financial criteria are, to some degree, mode of payment specific. Company subscribers are mainly concerned to collect their money's worth and achieve value for money. For individual and non-subscribers minimizing the financial cost is more pertinent, as they bear increased premiums through use. However, this distinction appears to be diminishing as the financial criteria are becoming increasingly important for companies and this necessarily filters down to company subscribers. For example, one respondent who actually organized his company's scheme related how his company used an incentive policy to prevent use.

> 'We impose them [limits] ourselves as well, certain limitations – what we call risk management – to make sure certain people don't go to the London clinic for an ingrowing toenail. And also we give an incentive to people not to use the private medical scheme, but wherever they can to use the health service. Now this may be politically wrong, I don't know, but it keeps our premiums down. It is for our benefit to say to them, "Well, yes, OK if you go to the . . . NHS hospital instead of the . . . private hospital we will give you one hundred pounds a week tax free". So there is an incentive for them not to use it at all times. Very, very few people use it.'

Another felt that his company may be experiencing problems, as employees took advantage of the scheme.

> 'Well, I think there has been a number of things that people have been going in for, various things almost as though, not as though they have stored them up, but as the scheme has come

in the last few years. A lot of people are in the age bracket of the forties and fifties and at the stage where you might require the odd operation, so I heard it said by personnel informally that there has been quite a lot of demand and the premiums have gone up.'

Another told how the employees had been warned about over-use.

'They told us we might have to start paying something because people were taking advantage.'

One company had had to employ its own physiotherapist because claims for this service had been so high that it made financial sense to pay a salary rather than meet the premium increases. Thus, financial criteria are influential but vary in significance according to the mode of payment category.

Finally, decision-making can also be seen to be influenced by cash benefits or incentives by insurance companies to use the NHS. Certainly waiting was a recognized problem but subscribers weighed it against the advantage of cash payments from the insurers if they used the NHS. This benefited both parties. The patient got somewhere between £35 and £55 a day while the insurance company paid less than the cost of the hotel fees and the wages of the medical staff in the private sector. As one respondent remarked:

'The advantage is the cash benefits. If you are an NHS patient there is a cash benefit payable per day you are in hospital. It was one of the reasons we took it out.'

In this case it is the NHS which loses out by being involved in an intricate decision about use and effectively subsidizing that decision by offering a cheaper alternative for the insurance company.

### The influence of general practitioners

Decisions to use health services have been shown to be influenced by significant others (Calnan, 1987) such as relatives and friends. In the case of use of the private sector the lay referral system appears to have less significance than the influence of the GP. Indeed GPs in particular are often described as having a 'gatekeeper' role, in the sense that they suggest referral and can give or withhold information about possible routes.

'I never say anything. The doctor always says, "Well, look, you are in BUPA, so let's send you off". It's automatic . . . the minute anything happens they just whizz 'em off to see the specialist.'

'My doctor just looks at my card and says, "Alright, I am sending you off to such and such a doctor to have this done", so it was almost not a choice.'

The preferences of the GP can in some cases be observed by the respondent.

'My impression is that the GP is not too keen on the private sector. I have a feeling that some are more anti. My previous doctor used to rush me off without a thought. This one doesn't.'

At the same time, however, the holding of insurance supposedly confers on the individual the 'power' to demand alternatives and thus specific action from the GP (Harris and Seldon, 1987; Saunders and Harris, 1989). However, the 'competence gap' (Tuckett *et al.*, 1985) limits patient involvement and hence their input in medical decisions (Titmuss, 1969). This was fully expressed by the respondents in their accounts:

'He [GP] has got the power. There is no doubt about it, that you are usually in their hands. One of the things is that the punter doesn't know . . . I have got no idea who is the expert in this sort of thing. You might know to go to a particular shop or to buy a particular product . . . but you don't know this week's best buy in medical terms. You know *Consumer Which* don't do a "best specialist of the week".'

Of course some respondents may refer themselves without recourse to the GP, but this was the least likely option.

'A colleague of my wife said this chap was good and we should see him. I said, "Right we will". We rang up. We didn't go behind the GP's back we told him what we were doing.'

'I got the appointment [NHS] through and it was in eight months, so I phoned the secretary and asked for a private appointment and two days later saw the consultant.'

The majority of the respondents, however, were happy to let their GP make the decision (only two respondents, both subscribers, said they would override a decision made by the GP) and would accept treatment on the NHS if the GP suggested it. Many argued that the

GP would ask them if they had got insurance and then say, 'Well you may as well go privately'.

It was also suggested that having insurance may increase the likelihood of being referred.

> 'I suspect they will refer you on more if you've got PHI. I don't know whether they [GPs] have an agreement with the consultants.'

One respondent believed it was the ideas of the particular doctor that were important. His GP, for instance, liked to treat patients himself.

> 'My present doctor is disinclined to send you away. They are a profession and don't want to pass you on.'

Patients may also initiate a request for private referral from the GP, but this was also unlikely. When such demands were reported they illustrated that medical authority could be approached and questioned. Finally, under some schemes GP referral is necessary.

> 'Well, for private treatment under PPP, you need a referral from your GP. That's one of their stipulations.'

In contrast to the GP, hospital doctors appear to have a limited influence. Only one respondent referred to initiation of private medicine coming from the consultant, suggesting this is a less important influence.

> *Respondent*:  'She [subscriber's wife] had been referred by the GP to the consultant and he pointed out to her that the waiting list was tremendously long in the NHS and to use the scheme.'
>
> *Interviewer*:  'What was the waiting list in the NHS?'
>
> *Respondent*:  'Well it could have been done in several weeks because there was a threat of cancer . . . I guess one has a twinge of being a bit unfair, because he was buying a place in the queue.'

This section has clearly established the importance of the GP (although not the consultant) in the decision to use the private sector. Private medical insurance therefore does not seem to confer autonomy and power for many subscribers; rather advice from medical personnel seems to be accepted. We can summarize why this may be the case.

*Incapacitation.* The illness state itself can make decision-making problematic in that patients feel vulnerable and behave passively.
*Inadequate knowledge base.* In the same way as respondents have limited knowledge about waiting lists, they do not have adequate information about consultants, hospital times and the 'best' place to go.
*Deference to medical personnel.* It could be that the medical profession commands a position of superiority strengthened by their position as 'expert' in relation to the patient (Titmuss, 1969). However, this deference might decline once patients have gone private and want value for money. Evidence from observational studies (Silvermann, 1984) suggests that in consultations in the private sector patients are more challenging and doctors expect it.

## The designation of conditions as public or private

Analysis of our transcripts also revealed a logic in terms of which conditions were appropriate for the private or public sector. Interestingly, respondents varied in their perceptions in quite contradictory ways, illustrating the complexity of lay criteria. For example, some respondents believed the private sector was necessary for serious treatment and hospitalization.

'I'm not bothered with the private, I didn't think I was sufficiently bad enough.'

Others believed the private sector should concentrate on the 'trivia' of medicine – those small unnecessary or cosmetic operations which were seen to overload the NHS. Still others saw the remit of the NHS as being to provide costly treatment which would boost premiums to unaffordable levels if available privately, e.g. GP and casualty services.

'It's a terrible thing to say but it's like car insurance. Once you start using them, they load up the premiums. So have it done on the NHS and keep the prices down. I sound terribly mercenary.'

It was also recognized by many that the private sector is limited in that only certain conditions are covered. Pre-existing conditions are often excluded and those conditions treated by the private sector involve cheaper, profit-making operations.

'She [the GP] said, "Did you know, if you belong to BUPA, if you go private and have renal problems, they won't reinsure you afterwards?" So PHI is alright up to a point but you certainly need the NHS as a back-up because they don't cater for chronically or terminally ill. They [PHI] might do minor or major operations like hip replacements. You pay a lot of money and they don't cover you for everything. That's what I'm trying to say. Private medicine is used, to be blunt, in most cases to jump the queue for minor things. I don't bother going private since I did try to use it and they said it was an ongoing thing and I wasn't covered. Many of our colleagues have landed bills when they thought they were covered.'

Finally, of course, the private sector was seen as invaluable in non-emergency cases where the waiting list was long.

'My wife had one or two gynaecology problems that required fairly prompt treatment but did not come into the category of emergency demand in the NHS.'

Thus, the severity of medical problems and concerns about the extent of cover are involved in the decision to make use of the private sector.

## Benefits of private care and problems with the NHS

We also investigated whether the perceived benefits of the private sector influenced the decisions to use it. Were differences expressed about the public and private sectors in terms of delivery and standard of care? The majority did not recognize such differences in terms of technical care and this is supported by the preparedness of all respondents to use the NHS if the need arose.

'The care in the end is very much the same. You have the same surgery, same drugs, same surgeon, maybe he will give you more time on his rounds.'

The main benefits, as we might expect, were speed and convenience. Beyond these creature comforts, other aspects were recognized as superior in the private sector.

'Private hospital treatment is superb, you get a private room, you get tea, you get waited on hand and foot. Everything is first class which is what you expect if you are paying for it.'

Dissatisfaction with the standard of care in the NHS can also be important. In particular, it was non-subscribers who decided to pay for private treatment who most clearly articulated such explanations, either because of waiting or dissatisfaction with other aspects of the care. Their decision was seldom automatic except for one man who preferred the quality of the private sector (and the type of patient) but could not get an insurance company to cover him because of pre-existing conditions. Otherwise calculated reasoning prevailed as the following response illustrates:

'I am totally against the idea of private medicine in principle but when it comes down in practice to making sure my family is OK, then I will pay. We were very dissatisfied [with the son's treatment on the NHS]. His [doctor's] whole manner was wrong. Perhaps he had an off day. The private chap was different, spent much more time talking to us . . . maybe it's down to the individual personality as well.'

Generally, the majority of respondents did see these aspects as largely superficial and acknowledged that in some cases the NHS provided such care. At the same time, problems experienced with the private sector were recognized. Loneliness, the expense and unnecessary operations were all mentioned and seemed likely to influence future decisions about whether or not to use their insurance:

'I almost liked the NHS better, there were more people about. You feel a bit lonely in the private and the food was far too cordon bleu . . . too rich. My impression was that the bills were marked up unrealistically. I was amazed at the cost of some things.'

*Principles*

Finally, respondents' principles, both political and moral, seemed to influence decisions. These were clearly illustrated in a number of accounts, particularly from company subscribers, and relate directly to their non-use of the private sector. The following extract comes from a company subscriber.

*Interviewer*: 'Did you think about not accepting it [PHI] when it was given?'
*Respondent*: 'I just ignored it.'
*Interviewer*: 'Would you use it?'
*Respondent*: 'No – it milks the NHS, it takes away a lot of good doctors. In general it just takes away and gets you to the head of the queue and everybody else down.'

What, then, are the implications of this analysis for understanding why and when people used their insurance or conversely why and when they did not? Of particular interest was whether the subscription to private health insurance did actually extend the choice of options for consumers. The answer to this appears to be that choice is extended only slightly. Certainly, according to the survey data, the majority of subscribers did use their private health insurance, although the private sector tended to be used as a substitute rather than a complement to NHS hospital services. That is, shopping around between the private sector and the public sector was only undertaken by a minority of users. Decisions about whether or not to use the private sector tended to be influenced by resource issues such as concerns about time and finance, with subscribers weighing up the costs and benefits of use. However, for other users such calculated reasoning was not in evidence and decisions were automatic or routine either because of dissatisfaction with the NHS or simply out of habit. For them, the priority was to get value for money. Certainly, those who experienced private health care did emphasize the quality of the facilities as well as the individualized aspects of care. However, the extent to which private health insurance conferred choice and autonomy was limited because there were a series of barriers to its use – three major and one minor. Of the major barriers, one of these was ideological; for many subscribers there was a strong political and moral commitment to the NHS which appeared to inhibit their use of the private sector. This is a finding which has been regularly found in surveys which have shown strong public support for the NHS as an institution. The second major barrier is financial. This applied to the individual subscribers in particular who had to weigh up the benefits of circumventing waiting lists with the risks that their premiums increased if they used it. This concern about increased premiums appears now to be extended to employer-run schemes where there is pressure on employees to ration use.

The other major barrier to the use of private health insurance is the GP who not only acts as the gatekeeper for patient access to NHS hospital services but also appears to perform a similar function for private hospital services. Patients rarely bypass the GP and appear to be content to let him or her make the decision about where they are referred. The GP, therefore, acts as an intermediary between the patient and the private sector and the latter is dependent upon the NHS for its referrals. The passivity of the patients in our study may be due to inadequate knowledge about the best doctor or hospital and the extent of their insurance cover for their condition, their incapacitation due to illness or general deference to medical authority. Once the GP was given the authority to make the decision, non-medical as well as medical considerations appeared to influence the eventual outcome. Certainly, there was little evidence of GPs routinely having knowledge about whether their patient was covered by private insurance.

In addition, one barrier which appeared to be of lesser importance was the perceived remit of the private sector. Certain conditions were designated public or private, although there was considerable variation amongst respondents and these were again influenced by time and cost factors. The respondents clearly had a high regard for the NHS and saw certain, particularly more major, conditions better served by the public sector because of the facilities and expertise. While certain conditions were recognized as the preserve of the private sector this was not because of the belief that technical care would be better, but rather for reasons of speed, comfort and the belief that they were reducing waiting lists.

As we have suggested, these barriers limit the power of the consumer and therefore the notion of consumer sovereignty. The power of the GP in decision-making works against the idea that the consumer is freely able to shop around. Furthermore, we have also shown that our respondents had limited knowledge about their insurance cover and the costs of treatment which further raises doubts about their being well-informed and critical consumers.

Finally, there was evidence to suggest that there was some variation in use of private health service by mode of payment for private health insurance. Our analysis suggested that this may be explained by political principles and financial commitments. The individual subscribers were to some extent more pro-private, although we have shown this to be at the level of specific beliefs only, rather than broad political alignment. However, they paid individually for any increased costs incurred through use. This would explain the lower reported utilization of the private sector. It also explains the relatively high degree of commitment to, and reliance upon, the NHS purely because on some occasions they had to use the NHS if money was an issue. Thus, loyalty remains as the option if leaving the NHS is not available. Employer-paid subscribers were strongly anti-private but appeared to use their insurance more readily because there was no financial cost to bear and they were concerned to get their money's worth, particularly if the insurance was introduced as part of a wage deal. The joint subscribers fell somewhere in between. They may have had greater political affiliation with the private sector than company subscribers and expressed dissatisfaction with the NHS and were committed to the private sector as they made a contribution to the cost. At the same time, financial considerations associated with use were not as pertinent as increasing premiums were jointly met.

# 5

# PRIVATE HEALTH INSURANCE AS A CONSUMPTION GOOD

The previous chapters have focused on both the decision to take out private health insurance and the decision to use it. This chapter, drawing on some of the evidence presented previously, looks at a wider issue concerning the social meaning of private health insurance and whether subscription to private health insurance reflects a certain social position and with it a specific set of political attitudes and cultural perceptions. This question relates to a range of issues raised within the general debate about the new sociology of consumption.

One of the basic arguments used by the proponents of the sociology of consumption (Saunders, 1978, 1986, 1989; Dunleavy and Husbands, 1985) is that social divisions may be more usefully explored by concentrating on divisions associated with the sphere of consumption rather than production. However, there is some disagreement about the relative importance of consumption divisions compared with class divisions. For example, Saunders (1986, 1989) emphasizes that the analysis of social divisions should centre on the dimension of personal ownership (autonomy and control) which is independent of class divisions. Dunleavy and Husbands (1985), in contrast, suggest an interrelationship between class and consumption, noting that in some situations sectoral divisions cut across class lines whereas in others they are derived from class divisions. However, both sets of writers agree that divisions in the consumption sector between those people reliant on the state for housing, transport and health and welfare services and those who satisfy their requirements through the private market do shape political attitudes and cultural perceptions.

Much of the discussion around this issue has either been theoretical in nature or based on findings regarding private consumption in the area of housing (Hamnett, 1989). In the health field the main contribution has come from Busfield (1990) who has explored the implications of changes in the consumption of health care for social divisions through a secondary analysis of the General Household Survey.

In this chapter the aim is to explore the debate about health-care consumption further by examining three questions which have emerged from the new sociology of consumption. The first of these is whether the decision to opt for a 'privatized form of health provision' (private health insurance) signifies new social divisions which are independent of, or related to, class. Closely related to this is whether consumption location shapes political ideologies.

The second question focuses on the issue of the 'culture of consumption' and whether the introduction of the market economy into health care not only confers on the 'customer' purchasing power but also autonomy and freedom of choice. For example, is there any evidence of consumers of private health care 'shopping around' for health care?

Finally, the third question concerns the cultural significance of private health insurance and whether it is similar to other forms of consumption good. Clearly, certain types of consumer good have a status over and above their material value and this analysis focuses on how private health insurance is perceived in relation to other types of good.

## A NEW SOCIAL CLEAVAGE?

Do people who subscribe to private health insurance hold a distinct set of political beliefs and ideologies? In order to throw light on this question our interviewees were asked about their views on the following issues: private education; private pensions; the selling of council houses; the growth of private homes for the elderly and disabled; privatization of industries including utilities such as gas and water; and the contracting out of transport, cleaning and refuse collection services by local councils. If the sample of subscribers and non-subscribers hold similar views about each of these issues it would provide grounds for questioning the proposition that private health insurance can be used to explain social divisions, at least in terms of political beliefs and ideologies.

The first part of the analysis focused on identifying the range (if any) of ideologies used by the sample respondents. The second part focused on the variation (if any) by type of subscriber.

*Three* distinct ideologies emerged from the analysis. These stressed (i) individual responsibility for health and welfare, (ii) state responsibility for provision of services, and (iii) joint responsibility between state and individual. Each of the three ideologies will be considered in turn.

**Ideologies**

*Individual responsibility and choice*

The importance of individual responsibility, choice, and personal control – values placed on both competition and home ownership and the constraining influence of the state – were key elements in this set of ideological beliefs. These aspects are well illustrated in the following respondents' accounts, beginning with individual initiative, choice and responsibility. From an individual subscriber:

> 'This Government has given the individual initiative. It has been made clear to us that if we want to get on in this life we've got to do the job.'

From a respondent receiving company insurance:

> 'I'm always a believer that the consumer should be powerful, you know the consumer should be the one to determine what is provided. Health is an unusual commodity, isn't it? I should like to think the consumer would be able to determine but at the end of the day I don't think they can. How do you judge? You can only do it after the event, but you can choose private. I think I should be permitted within the realms of legality to spend money on what I wish.'

Privatization and competition are illustrated by the following quotes from an individual subscriber and a company-based subscriber, respectively:

> 'Privatization means good healthy competition.'

> 'The private sector is efficient, accountable and apolitical.'

The benefits of the privatization of welfare services are illustrated by the following, the first two by individual subscribers, the third from a non-subscriber and the last from a company-based subscriber:

'Private education is much better than state education, it offers choice.'

'Don't know why we had council houses in the first place! Private everything apart from the National Health!'

'Private pensions are a great idea. State does not provide enough.'

'Owning your own home allows you to be master of your own destiny.'

## State responsibility

This ideology identifies the state as entirely responsible for the provision of services and determining individual needs. The state is perceived as the most appropriate provider as health and welfare services are best not left to the market and the state can ensure that the population as a whole receive services and can minimize inequalities. Once again these different aspects are clearly illustrated in the respondents' accounts, beginning with the state portrayed as paternalistic provider from a non-subscriber:

'The state is responsible for health. I think it is a total shame that all these things that were and are run by the Government are being privatized like water, electricity and by the sound of it, health. I don't think it is a good idea at all. The idea of a caring state is good. Private companies' idea – to make profits.'

'Government has got to organize health and education because it has to look after the ones who can't take care of themselves. Private poaches off the rest. Selling of council houses is absolutely criminal! You can give people assistance to buy houses but that is politically motivated.'

The next series of quotes illustrate the role of the state and the reduction of inequalities. From a company-based subscriber:

'The private sector weakens the public. Privatizing education is bad for the community. It splits it up, it stratifies it, it divides it.'

From a non-subscriber:

'All the changes just divide rich and poor.'

They also highlight the state's role as the provider of basic needs. From an individual subscriber:

'Health, education and water should be more public than anything else.'

From a company-based subscriber:

'Government should have control of all basics.'

### The public–private mix

The third ideological type which emerged through the analysis sees the responsibility for health and welfare as lying with both the state and the individual. It does not designate either the state or the individual as being more important but sees some services as being more applicable for the state to provide than others. This approach is characterized, first, by the need for joint responsibility, as the following respondents' accounts illustrate. From an individual, company-based and non-subscriber, respectively:

'The individual is primarily responsible, the Government is responsible to ensure a system exists.'

'It's the state's responsibility to produce the means and it's up to the individual to look after themselves. In a democratic society you have to have both public and private, but the state should be leading the way.'

'We are all responsible, but the state should be responsible too.'

Second, this ideology is exemplified by a preference for a mixed economy in terms of provision. From a company-based and individual subscriber, respectively:

'Competition if it's not an essential service.'

'Selling council houses? OK, so long as you build more for those unable to buy.'

### Summary

Classifying the data in this way provides the basis for making the following observations. First, no respondent fitted exactly into any ideology. Instead they combined strands from at least two of the ideologies during the interview (or while discussing a particular question). Not only was such juggling exhibited in many pro-privatization comments about health; it was also apparent in talk about selling council houses. Again respondents drew on two or three ideologies simultaneously or used one or the other in responding to different questions. Second, holding strands from all three types of ideology did not necessarily mean everyone fell into the third type. The third type of ideology is where the respondent sees the state and private sectors working together in specific areas simultaneously.

Were any of these three types of political ideology more prevalent among one or other of the groups of private health insurance subscribers? Overall there was not any clear evidence of differences between the groups although subscribers more often referred to individual responsibility than non-subscribers. However, it was in relation to specific issues that differences were more in evidence. While there was general antagonism towards private health care amongst almost the whole sample, irrespective of subscription to private health insurance, differences did emerge in relation to private education. Individual subscribers favoured private education whereas non-subscribers were fervently anti-private education because it was 'snobbish' and 'divisive'.

In summary, the analysis so far suggests that private health insurance is a weak indicator of new social divisions in that there is little evidence that subscription to private health insurance was associated with a distinct set of political beliefs and ideologies. Certainly, in relation to health care, there appeared to be a consensus amongst the sample as a whole that it was a basic service which the state should provide, although there was less of a consensus about other areas of welfare.

## ESTABLISHING THE PATIENT AS 'CUSTOMER'

The second question in this chapter examines whether having access to private health care through private health insurance gives consumers choice and autonomy in their pattern of health-care use. The data collected in this study enabled this question to be examined in a number of different ways. First, there is the issue of perceived choice which was addressed by talking to the respondents directly about the degree of perceived choice available in the selection of specialists and hospitals. Their comments suggest the choice had been made mainly by the GP:

'I didn't choose the hospital or doctor. The GP made the choice.'

'Doctors are talking about something that most people have little knowledge about anyway.'

'From experience I shouldn't have any choice. If I want private treatment I'm in the private establishment.'

Only 5 out of 28 users argued they had a choice of consultant and hospital. As one of them argued:

'You have a choice of hospital and consultant. I chose the one I felt happier with. I think in the earlier days I used to leave it up to the GP, but I think now probably with the business, I spend more time on considerations of this and knowing a lot of people here particularly locally in the medical scene. I'm an avid reader of the medical directory actually to see what qualifications people have got . . .'

This last quotation was the only one of this kind and the respondent was different in that his son had a brain tumour and was under constant treatment. Thus this man had lots of contacts and technical knowledge. Furthermore, his other son was a doctor.

When it came to choice of time, more positive comments were expressed and it was in this context that choice was most clearly articulated.

'Choice is getting something done quicker.'

'It's the immediacy of response that is important.'

Thus, again, speed and timing and jumping the queue were the most important criteria for the respondents. It is interesting to note that the choice of consultant and hospital was rarely mentioned voluntarily. Rather, it was only in response to direct questioning and then in a negative way, suggesting choice in these terms was not an important issue or a reality. Thus, choice was absent from the respondents' discourse, except in relation to timing and speed.

Non-users and non-subscribers were turned to next to elicit what they thought about *choice* in the private sector.

'I would expect people to dance if I went private. I demand good service when I am "shopping" and were I in need of an operation I am "shopping", there's no difference. In principle I would expect people to jump around and look interested.'

It was argued by one non-subscriber that choice was available on the NHS, if you demanded it.

'You can get choice in the NHS if you ask. I think it is a lot easier to choose a time but people are frightened to ask.'

Likewise, a company subscriber suggested:

'It doesn't make me feel more of a customer. I pay my NI and I am a customer and I am just as entitled to that care . . . by being a paying member of the NHS as I am by being private.'

Again choice of consultant and hospital was not a noted advantage of the private sector. Non-respondents did not talk in terms of 'choice' in any way except timing. The private sector then confers choice but only in terms of timing.

Second, there is the question of the actual pattern of utilization behaviour which shows that, in reality, choice is rather limited. In Chapter 4 it was shown that respondents tended to use one sector or the other and there was little evidence of respondents using a mix of both sectors. However, shopping around was evident, at least, in terms of decision-making. Patients did weigh up the advantages and disadvantages of the different options although it was not manifest in actual behaviour in that many consistently chose in the same way. Resource concerns (i.e. time and money) were the major criteria on which decisions were made. Also, as was suggested previously, patients are largely referred to private medical care by GPs and in terms of decision-making the role of the GP is fundamental in influencing patients' pathways to private health care. For many subscribers, then, private medical insurance clearly did not confer autonomy and power. Rather, advice from medical personnel was more influential. This may be due to the special qualities associated with health care, such as the inadequate knowledge base of respondents, or it may be that illness itself can induce passivity. Higgins (1988) also points out that patients' choice of hospital and consultant is limited in that the patient may choose the hospital or the consultant but not both.

The study also highlights other constraints on choice. One of these was the lack of knowledge expressed by the subscribers about the cost of treatment and the extent to which this limited the care covered by the policy. Subscribers, then, do not appear to have the information which would empower them to be 'enterprising' and 'critical' consumers. In addition, evidence presented previously (see Chapter 3) suggests that the decision to take out private health insurance was not always an individual choice but a 'perk' or gift bestowed by employers.

## DESIGNATION AS A CONSUMPTION GOOD

### The value of private health insurance

This third section is designed to ascertain whether private health insurance can be designated as a consumption good. It has been argued (Titmuss, 1969) that medical care is qualitatively different from other types of good which are purchased in the market context, because prospective users have no way of knowing how much medical care will be needed in the future. This question was not addressed directly in the study although the data shed some light on whether medical care provided by private health insurance has distinctive qualities or whether it is similar to other consumption goods. More specifically, respondents' accounts were examined in terms of the following:

1 Status of private health insurance as a consumer good
2 Status of the person who subscribes to private health insurance
3 Value attached to private health insurance
4 Value attached to private health insurance compared with other consumption goods.

Each of these issues is important in that it gives clues to the social weight and value placed on private health insurance as perceived by the respondents and, thereby, the extent to which it may be defined as a consumption good.

### *Private health insurance as a status symbol*

There was no evidence of a widespread belief amongst the sample that private health insurance was a status symbol. Some suggested that it had once been so but deemed that this was no longer the case because of it now being more widely available. From an individual subscriber:

> 'I don't think it's a status symbol. Plenty of working class people have it.'

For some people it even had negative connotations, as this non-subscriber:

> 'I wouldn't see it as a status symbol. I'd feel guilty about it.'

The minority who did regard private health insurance as a status symbol did tend to be non-subscribers:

> 'Yes it is. It's a nice thing to drop into conversation, I'd like to meet you but I'm off to my clinic for my annual health check.'

Those that did subscribe did not see it as a status symbol for themselves but recognized it could have this potential in the eyes of others:

> 'Some people have it for status, keeping up with the Joneses.'

> 'It is a status symbol, as well as a lot of other things. Some of my colleagues at work who weren't in private medicine prior to last year when the present company gave us insurance used to say, "It's terrible". The moment it was paid for by the company they rushed at it and I think they regard it as slightly, how shall I put it, one up on the guy next door who can't afford it.'

In summary, there was ambivalence about the status of private health insurance. Although subscribers and non-subscribers said that it had a social value, they were negative about those who adhered to this status.

## Type of person who is a subscriber

The status of a consumption good appears to be associated not only with the nature of the commodity itself but also with 'the type of person' who purchases it. Was there any evidence of such a stereotyped image (either positive or negative) being associated with private health insurance? A large number said it was impossible to identify such a typical person nowadays because of the wide social

spectrum of people who are subscribers, as this individual subscriber:

> 'I don't associate private health insurance with anyone. I'm just
> a normal working guy.'

Others, however, felt it was still possible to identify a type of person
and distinguished them on grounds such as socio-economic group
membership, political values and principles and the importance
attached to health. From a company-based subscriber:

> 'I associate it with financially stable people, professional rather
> than industrial.'

And an individual subscriber:

> 'Those that take it out are those with a priority for health not
> necessarily wealthy. You can make economies if you want to.'

Thus, despite the increase in the number and 'range' of people
holding insurance, it was possible for the respondents to identify
certain characteristics of typical holders and non-holders of insurance. Interestingly, these data suggest the need to be cautious about
drawing conclusions about private health insurance as a status
symbol as they show that a number of the respondents felt 'class'
was important and incorporated status-type arguments into their
responses. Thus, at a public level respondents may state that private
health insurance has little importance as a status symbol whereas at
the private level, in unstructured discourse, its status connotations
may be more apparent.

*Private health insurance as a luxury or necessity*

What value did those participating in the research place on private
health insurance? In this section, respondents' comments about
whether private health insurance is a luxury or necessity are described. This should give clues as to whether private health insurance is seen as a commodity.

The evidence shows that respondents had different perceptions
of the value of private health insurance according to whether they
were subscribers or not. Individual subscribers were the only respondents to describe private health insurance as an absolute
necessity:

'I look upon it as a necessity as I'm the breadwinner.'

The other two groups were more likely to see private health insurance as a luxury, as this company-based subscriber:

'Oh it is a luxury, definitely a luxury. I could happily exist and bring up my family without it.'

However, some were doubtful about the distinction between luxury and necessity, as these two company-based subscribers:

'It's not a luxury or necessity, it's convenience.'

'It's not a luxury you skimp and save for – it's not a necessity either. You get reasonable treatment in the NHS . . . It's almost like a conscious investment.'

Perception of the value placed on private health insurance is, according to this evidence, shaped by whether the respondent is personally a subscriber or not. Clearly, for the individual subscriber, material interests (e.g. being self-employed) shape the meaning attached to it, in that private health insurance is like any other commodity which influences his material circumstances.

## The substitutability of private health insurance

In this final section the value put on private health insurance is examined in terms of what the subscribers said they would give up to continue to subscribe to it. This involves looking at whether other goods would be substituted in favour of private health insurance and what sort of goods these would be.

Not surprisingly the value placed on private health insurance as a luxury or necessity shaped respondents' perceptions of its substitutability. Those individual subscribers who had described private health insurance as a necessity said they were prepared to make 'sacrifices' to continue use.

'I would sacrifice most things to keep insurance except school fees, for example, continental holidays. It's a necessity.'

'If it [premium] increased dramatically it would go, but I would forego luxuries like a holiday abroad . . . it's essential.'

Individual subscribers who saw private health insurance as a luxury, however, said they might forego spending on certain items although they clearly valued it less.

'I think it's a luxury, personally. I would forego spending on one or two meals out, I don't think I would spend less on my holiday because that's important for health reasons.'

The majority of company subscribers said they would not forego spending for private health insurance, or substitute it for another good. Indeed many said they had not wanted it in the first place but that it had been given to them and so they had taken it.

'I would drop it. I wouldn't look for it in a new job. I'd prefer a better pension.'

Non-subscribers were asked what they would spend any extra money on and the majority did not identify private health insurance as being desirable.

'If you've got money it's the sort of thing you invest in, but I'd buy other things first.'

**Summary**

In summary, the desirability of private health insurance as a 'consumption good' is clearly dependent upon individuals' priorities and the meaning health insurance holds for them. Only for individual subscribers was it seen as a necessity and as something which would not be willingly substituted. For the remainder of the sample, private health insurance was seen as a good which had some attractions but was not seen as being necessary to meet immediate needs.

What, then, are the implications of this analysis for the propositions which have emerged recently amongst advocates of the sociology of consumption? One of the most important propositions adopted by commentators has been that social divisions may be more usefully explored by concentrating on divisions associated with the sphere of consumption rather than production. This approach to the 'new' social divisions has been questioned by, amongst others, Hamnett (1989) who argues that 'class' still has explanatory power at the aggregate level, if not in individual cases. The qualitative research reported here, while not enabling an examination of the 'class' question directly in terms of class-related beliefs, has revealed specific intra-class beliefs and values associated with the 'consumption' of private health insurance.

A number of observations emerged from the analysis which have implications for the debate about a new social cleavage. The first is that consumption of private health insurance has little power to explain or account for the 'new' social divisions. While there was evidence in respondents' accounts of support for the values associated with neo-liberalism (Harris and Seldon, 1987) the use of this ideology was not confined to subscribers to private health insurance. In fact, there was evidence that respondents 'juggled' with more than one type of ideology and the use of ideology seemed to be related to specific issues. Certainly, respondents tended not to operate with a 'New Right' or a mixed economy ideology when they discussed the topic of health care. This appears to confirm the view that health and health care have special qualities (Titmuss, 1969) that distinguish them from other services and goods. It also explains why subscribers tended to express different ideological views to non-subscribers when discussing other welfare issues.

Second, it is possible to comment on another proposition from the new sociology of consumption which sees privatized forms of service delivery enabling a change in the status of the health service user from passive patient to active, enterprising customer. Saunders (1989) has argued that only marketization and commodification forms have this quality and recognized that these forms were underdeveloped. However, little evidence was found in the study reported here, at least as regards private health care, to support any marked increase in the availability of choice, autonomy and freedom. The majority of respondents, whilst feeling they gained an increase in choice in terms of timing as well as more individualized care, did not feel more empowered or more knowledgeable and there was little evidence of the enterprising customer 'shopping around'. Thus, choice might be expressed in theory but not in the actual health service utilization patterns of the users. However, the evidence presented here was limited to men and further research should examine women's patterns of utilization as they tend to be heavier users of private health care (Wiles, 1993).

Finally, the analysis casts light on the status and value attached to private health insurance as a consumption good. The evidence shows that private health insurance, as perceived by respondents, had a social significance over and above its function. Despite denials of status connotations for themselves, respondents tended to describe insurance in social terms. These data suggest that particular beliefs and values are associated with private health care but they also highlight the relationship between private health insurance and class, income and occupation. One implication of this is that the consumption of private health care might be a symbol of socio-economic position rather than a substitute for it.

In conclusion, the evidence from this study adds weight to the claims of those who have argued that private medical care challenges the proposition that divisions of consumption have replaced divisions of production. Busfield (1990) argues that theories of consumption are of little value on the grounds that most people are both private and public consumers of health care. This study provides some support for Busfield's argument, although the level of commuting between similar services in the NHS and the private sector was not high. Furthermore, the data suggest that beliefs and ideologies about health care are consistent across subscribers and non-subscribers. They also show that consumption of private health care is associated with images of class and status, suggesting that it may be more useful to see private health insurance as an indicator of social class rather than a substitute for it.

# 6

# CONCLUSION

The last decade has witnessed a significant increase in the size of the UK private health-care sector. Private hospitals and hospital beds have increased dramatically and subscriptions have grown year on year. Those who have sought to explain these developments have generally concentrated on the supply side and the role of the state, insurance companies, private hospitals and doctors. As a result surprisingly little consideration has been given to the role of users or 'consumers' of health care. Most of the research which has been carried out in this area has involved using surveys to establish whether the growth in private medicine reflects consumer dissatisfaction with the NHS. While providing a useful starting point for understanding the user's perspective such an approach, however, tells us little about the decision-making processes which lead people to take out insurance and influence whether they subsequently use it.

The study reported in this book has tried to address these issues. Drawing on interview data and to a lesser extent postal survey data collected for a local study of subscribers and non-subscribers of private health insurance in Kent, we have tried to provide answers to questions such as the following:

- Is there a typical subscriber?
- Why are decisions made to subscribe to or use such insurance?
- What social meanings are attached to it and do these reflect specific political beliefs and cultural perceptions?

The first of these issues was considered in Chapter 2. On the basis of an analysis of survey evidence from our local study and from national studies we suggested that there is a 'typical' subscriber with a distinct set of views about private health care and specific socio-political beliefs which differ from those of non-subscribers. More specifically, subscribers appear to be more dissatisfied with the NHS, and these views in turn seem to be related to broader socio-political values which emphasize a minimal role for state intervention and prioritize individual responsibility for health and health care. In the light of such beliefs it is not surprising that those who hold them should be the stronger supporters of a mixed economy of health care.

In Chapter 3 these findings were put to the test by drawing on in-depth interviews with subscribers and non-subscribers to private health insurance. We found that the survey results which suggested that dissatisfaction with the NHS is a major reason for subscribing to private health insurance is misleading and that such dissatisfaction does not necessarily affect subscribers' broad principles about the organization and funding of the health-care system. People appear to hold private health insurance for a number of reasons. Two of these are related to the supply side, where the employer gives the insurance as a 'perk' and where the very existence of a mixed economy of health care means that people use it. Another three factors relate to the demand side. Private health insurance is taken out because of the perceived advantage in terms of the social relations of health care, especially more individualized treatment. It is also felt to minimize the risk of not being treated immediately and the consequent loss of time and money caused by being placed on an NHS waiting list. And it is seen as a rational response to the perceived risk of deterioration in the subscriber's or other family member's health status.

Whatever the pragmatic reasoning, however, this did not seem to undermine their support for the principle of a health service for all 'free' of charge. While they recognized the advantages of private medicine they also continued to support the principles behind the NHS. Such 'ambivalence' has been noted by others and has been explained in a variety of ways. For Taylor-Gooby (1987), support for both public and private sectors is explained by self-interest. There is support for the state service because it is beneficial, but also an endorsement of the legitimacy of the market as this is the basis of consumption in a capitalist society. Exit from the NHS and support for the private sector depends on the balance of state and private provision. While lack of subsidies to the private health sector limits enrolment, the nature of capitalism and capitalist ideology ensure support for market principles and privatization. Thus, according to

Taylor-Gooby, it is self-interest which ensures support for the NHS and private health care and the belief that the private sector offers better facilities is not in opposition to support for state services.

A second interpretation for this 'ambivalence' has been offered by Saunders and Harris (1989). For them strong support for state welfare, as well as the private sector, is an artefact of the structure of social provision. Because people are obliged to pay taxes for state health care, choice is pre-empted. It is therefore rational for them to express opinions which appear to support both systems. However, Saunders and Harris argue that this ambivalence should not be interpreted as evidence of popular support for the state. The reason for such a combination of views is the lack of choice offered by the state, not the choice offered by the market as Taylor-Gooby would argue.

A further explanation is put forward by Busfield (1990). She suggests that support for both sectors arises because people consume both. Those with private health insurance are rarely covered for primary and chronic care and thus have to use the NHS. Consequently, they support the state sector because of material self-interest.

Our data suggest that Busfield comes closest to explaining this ambivalence. Those of our respondents who purchased private health insurance (half had been 'given' it by their employers) did not do so because of a commitment to the market and did not support the NHS because of a lack of choice. They decided to subscribe on pragmatic grounds, because of the lack of waiting and the perceived level of comfort offered by the private sector. Thus, while Busfield rightly notes that support for the state is dependent on practical considerations, we have shown that the same applies when it comes to support for the private sector. Our respondents were pro-NHS in *principle* but took out private health insurance for practical reasons, while resenting the fact that they had to pay twice and wishing they could get the service that they wanted from the NHS. This is quite different from Saunders's (1989) view that people resent paying twice because they feel they are 'trapped consumers' and see the private sector as their 'ideal preference'.

In Chapter 4 we shifted the focus of attention from the decision to take out private health insurance to the decision to use it. This is important because, while the great majority of users of private health care have insurance cover, it appears that a considerable proportion do not use it and that some of these stop paying as a result. To what extent, then, do people use private health insurance, when do they do so and does it extend 'consumer choice'? According to our survey data, the majority of subscribers did use their insurance although they used the private sector as a substitute for, rather than as a complement to, the NHS. Thus, only a minority of patients appeared to 'shop around' for care between the two sectors.

For many subscribers the decision to use the private sector was influenced by pragmatic considerations like time and money. Others routinely decided to use the private sector because of dissatisfaction with the NHS or out of habit, for the priority was to obtain 'value for money'. Some of this variation in the use of private medicine was related to the mode of payment for private health insurance. While individual subscribers were to some extent more pro-private at the level of specific beliefs, they reported using the private sector less than other subscribers because they paid individually for any increased costs incurred through use. Employer-paid subscribers were more strongly anti-private but appeared to use their insurance more readily because there was no financial cost to bear and they were concerned to get their money's worth, especially if their insurance was introduced as part of a wage deal. The joint subscribers took a position midway between these two. While they were politically more in sympathy with private health care than company subscribers and more committed because they contributed to the cost, they were not affected by the prospect of increasing premiums as individual subscribers because costs were met jointly.

Did the use of private health insurance increase 'consumer choice'? The answer seems to be that choice was extended only slightly. Certainly those who had experienced private health care stressed the quality of the facilities and the individualized nature of care but there was, as we noted earlier, little shopping around between the private and public sector.

Moreover, the extent to which private health insurance conferred choice and autonomy was restricted by a series of barriers. Of these the most important were ideology, money and the general practitioner. For many subscribers there was a strong moral commitment to the NHS which appeared to inhibit the use of the private sector. Others, particularly individual subscribers, were concerned about the cost of premiums and weighed up the benefits of side-stepping waiting lists against the risk that their premium might be increased if they used it. And other subscribers were restricted in their use of private hospital care by their GP who they appeared content to let decide whether or not they were referred. This passivity may be due to inadequate knowledge about the best doctor or hospital, or the extent of their insurance cover for their condition; or it might be a consequence of incapacitation due to illness or general deference to medical authority. Whatever the reasons, however, the effect of these barriers was to limit the power of the consumer and thus the notion of consumer sovereignty. The power of the GP in decision-making works against the principle of consumer choice while the respondents' limited knowledge of their insurance cover and the cost of treatment limits their opportunity to act as well-informed and critical consumers.

In Chapter 5 we broadened our approach and looked at the social meaning of private health insurance. In particular we tried to address three issues which relate to debates in the sociology of consumption. First, does the decision to opt for a privatized form of health provision signify new social divisions which are independent of, or related to, class and is such consumption associated with a particular political ideology? Second, has the introduction of a market economy for health care conferred on the 'customer' autonomy and freedom of choice as well as purchasing power? And third, is the cultural significance attached to private health insurance similar to other forms of consumption good?

On the first question our analysis provided little support for the proposition that the consumption of private health insurance highlights a social division which is independent of class. While there was some evidence of support for the neo-liberal strand of the New Right ideology this was not confined to subscribers to private health insurance and indeed this ideology was more often articulated when discussing other welfare issues than health and health care.

Likewise, our study provided little support for the view that the marketization and commodification of health care have resulted in greater choice, autonomy and freedom. Although the majority of our respondents said that private health insurance had given them more choice in terms of timing and more individualized care, they did not feel more empowered or more knowledgeable and gave little indication of 'shopping around'. Consequently, while there was some acknowledgement of greater choice in theory, this did not appear to be borne out in practice.

As for the question of the cultural significance of private health insurance, our respondents did attach social significance to it, like other commodities, but these values were also related to class, income and occupation. This suggests that the consumption of private health care is a symbol of socio-economic position rather than a substitute for it. Taken together, the evidence from Chapter 5 supports those who reject the proposition that divisions of consumption have replaced divisions of production. In the case of health care it seems that there is no clear division between consumers of public and private health care and the consumption of privatized provision is best seen as dependent on class rather than cutting across class lines.

We believe that these findings are of interest in their own right. However, they also have specific sociological and policy implications. In the remainder of this chapter we shall therefore outline what we believe these are, taking each area in turn.

## SOCIOLOGICAL IMPLICATIONS

We started this book by outlining a model for the lay evaluation of health care which assumed that people have their own complex criteria which provide the basis for their involvement in private health care. Our research can be used to evaluate this conceptual model. We argued that people have their own criteria for evaluating health care which the notion of 'patient satisfaction' fails to do justice to and that these provide a basis for their involvement with private health insurance. In particular, we suggested that people's perception of health care might be influenced by the following:

● the level and nature of their experience of health care and that of significant others
● the context-specific reasons for seeking help
● their socio-political values and the way these shape their perception of health care and how it should be used.

As we have seen, our research has confirmed the basic assumption of this model, namely that people who are active users of health services have clearly worked out criteria for evaluating the care provided. However, not all the elements of the model received equal support. There was little to suggest that the personal experience of health care provided people with a *raison d'être* for taking out and using private health insurance. Judgements about the quality of private health care seemed to depend primarily on hearsay, as did their views about the NHS.

On the other hand, socio-political beliefs played a major part in our respondents' evaluations. As noted in Chapter 3 there were few espousing an avowedly neo-liberal ideology; instead the great majority continued to express a strong attachment in principle to the egalitarian values underpinning the NHS when talking about health care. However, context-specific reasons seemed to intervene when it came to the practice of subscribing to or using private health care. Thus a perceived deterioration in health status or being self-employed and needing to make arrangements which minimized disruption to their jobs seemed to play a major role in determining how they related to private health care.

The analysis of subscribers' political beliefs and ideological preferences in Chapter 5 also enables us to comment on the nature of ideology. It suggests that people are far less consistent about their ideological position than many have supposed. Instead they seem to combine elements of different ideological positions simultaneously or in response to different questions. Thus our respondents combined elements from at least two different ideologies when talking about the provision of welfare services. This suggests that ideologies in general are not independently formulated ways of thinking but rather positions extracted from a single dialogue (Billig *et al.*, 1988).

Our discussion of the logic underpinning the decision to use private health insurance also has implications for the study of help-seeking behaviour. As we noted above, our respondents' decision whether or not to use their insurance tended to be influenced by calculating the costs and benefits of use, especially relating to resources such as time and money. At the same time, use was constrained by the existence of certain barriers such as a strong ideological commitment to the NHS. Neither of these issues has been given detailed consideration in previous studies of help seeking in the UK. The general absence of a cost–benefit model of decision-making may reflect these researchers' concern with state-funded health care and with patients who were only interested in temporal resources. Also, focusing on only one type of health-care system may have encouraged ideological issues to be taken for granted, especially if the system concerned involves professionals defining patient need as is the case with the NHS. As we have seen, ideological concerns may be central to the type of help-seeking behaviour chosen.

One aspect of help seeking which needs further consideration is that of gender. Our study has focused on men because they are the larger subscriber to private health insurance. As we noted in Chapter 5, however, women tended to be heavier users of private health insurance (Higgins and Wiles, 1992). They call on it to pay for gender-specific treatments which are inadequately covered under the NHS such as fertility clinics and abortion services (Higgins, 1988), and for universal treatments which are obtainable in both the public and private hospital acute sectors (Nicholl *et al.*, 1989b). Given this gender difference in utilization, there is a need to study the way in which the decision to use private health insurance is influenced by gendered perceptions of health-care need. Are women who can afford to do so actively choosing the private sector for inpatient care in preference to the NHS? Are the benefits which they identify different from those which the men reported in our study? To answer these questions, attention needs to be given to the consequences of women being the main carers of dependent family members, both young and old (Finch and Groves, 1983; Graham, 1984). Do women go private because being responsible for family health requires them to have maximum flexibility over admission dates? Do they see private medicine as providing them with the quality of care they need but do not get at home because they are the ones doing the caring? Do they see going private as enhancing the likelihood of a quick recovery and speedy return to their domestic and familial responsibilities? Some answers to these questions are found in a recent study (Wiles, 1993) which showed that while the reasons given by men and women for going private were similar, a closer examination revealed gender differences in their interpretations. These variations can be accounted for by the different socialization, social roles and social position of men.

In addition, consideration needs to be given to whether women decide to use private health care because they have found that NHS doctors are poorly equipped to deal with the unspecific complaints that they frequently present (Roberts, 1985) or have responded to their questions on the basis of negative gender stereotypes which has resulted in their condition not being taken seriously (Doyal and Elston, 1986). Are doctors working in the private health system perceived by women to take their condition more seriously and to give them more opportunity to discuss it than they would if they were being treated on the NHS? These concerns are clearly different to those of the men in our study who talked about flexible admission dates primarily in terms of the benefits for maximizing their earning power and saw quality of care as being to do with individualized treatment and not about getting doctors to treat their condition seriously.

The research reported here also has implications for our understanding of the nature of doctor–patient relations and medical authority. This relationship has traditionally been characterized in terms of professional dominance, with doctors controlling the consultation, and patients uncritically accepting their doctors' decisions because of their superior knowledge and skills (Friedson, 1970). For those who belong to the New Right, this relationship is primarily a consequence of the way the health-care system is funded. It is claimed that if the NHS was privately financed the relationship between doctors and patients would change on the grounds that 'whoever pays the piper calls the tune'. But how accurate is such an assessment? The evidence from our study suggests that private health insurance and health care has in fact done relatively little to empower consumers. There was little evidence of patients shopping around for the best treatment and subscribers seemed quite willing to accept their GPs' advice about where they should be referred. The only evidence of a more egalitarian relationship came from their accounts of the more individualized care offered by doctors working in private hospitals.

Of course there are limits to the inferences that can be drawn from such interview data, as the relationship between accounts and action is problematic. Observational research in NHS and private clinics by Silvermann (1984) however lends some support to our claim that a 'fee for service' system does not challenge medical authority in a fundamental way. He found that the private patients he observed continued to accept the technical dominance of the physician and accepted their role as lay people, lacking the knowledge to challenge their clinical judgements. At the same time, however, the private patients were far more likely to attempt to control the agenda of the consultation, introducing topics and asking the kinds of question not asked in NHS clinics.

Whether medical authority will continue to be accepted by patients receiving either private or public health care is however another matter. It has recently been argued that we are witnessing a major shift, if not a crisis, in the social relations of health care (Gabe and Bury, 1991) as a result of the increased questioning of medical knowledge and practice. Not only have we seen a new willingness on the part of doctors to criticize each other openly but these disputes have received maximum publicity through the mass media. Indeed this institution now occupies a strategic site on which conflicts about the social relations of health care are managed. Television is particularly important in this respect, providing an opportunity for claims-making activities by different interest groups and for journalists to create their own range of meanings through powerful image and narrative (Bury and Gabe, 1990). The media have in turn been used by consumer groups and self-help groups who have started to take a more active stance on health-care issues, including turning to lawyers in the hope of getting financial compensation for alleged medical negligence. Indeed, what were once matters of internal regulation by the medical profession are now frequently potential litigation issues, as the massive rise in doctors' defence insurance testifies (Ham *et al.*, 1988; Dingwall *et al.*, 1991). If the experience of doctors in the USA described by Annandale (1989) is anything to go by, any development of private health care in this country built on ideas about health care as a commodity and patients as consumers, is likely to see a further expansion of such litigation along with an undermining of medical authority.

Such a possibility, of course, also resonates with Giddens' (1990) claim that we are living in a period of high modernity in which the judgements of experts are constantly open to critical scrutiny and are either accepted or rejected by lay people on the basis of pragmatic calculations about the risks involved. To paraphrase Giddens (1991), in a system such as high modernity even the most cherished beliefs underpinning expert systems are open to revision and are regularly altered. In short, 'empowerment' is routinely available to lay people as part and parcel of the reflexive nature of high modernity.

Finally, we would like to comment on the likely prospects for the social meaning of private health insurance. As we noted earlier, our study has shown that such insurance has a social significance over and above its function but that the status connotations attached to it are a reflection of class position rather than a substitute for it. Whether this continues to be so is, however, an open question. If the emphasis on health as a commodity continues and ever more attention is given to the successful exercise of control over the self and management of the body (Crawford, 1984; Featherstone, 1987) it is possible that the status attached to having private health insurance will increase too, in so far as it is seen as representing a way of taking charge of one's health. Furthermore, this trend may be compounded by the growth of privatized living, with ever greater emphasis on individualized, family-centred activities, with its corresponding implications for social identity. In the light of such social processes it may be that greater value will be attached to private health insurance as a way of looking after 'the family's health'. Whether or not this is so, however, it seems unlikely that these meanings will become detached from class membership, as the opportunity to develop a healthy or privatized lifestyle is related to economic position (Navarro, 1991a). Thus we expect private health insurance to remain a status marker or 'positional good' (Hirsh, 1976; Featherstone, 1990) for middle-class professionals and managers which working-class people will be unable to usurp, primarily on financial grounds.

## POLICY IMPLICATIONS

Our research also has a number of policy implications. First, as noted earlier, it challenges the notion of consumer sovereignty favoured by those who advocate a 'market economy' approach to health care. Present Government policy is ostensibly based on the view that health is a commodity like other goods and services and that individuals should be allowed to determine the amount that they consume through the market, weighing up the advantages and disadvantages of a particular choice. The shift from 'patient' to 'consumer' was first enshrined in policy by the Griffiths management inquiry in 1983 (Allsop, 1992). The report argued that the interests of consumers should be central to all health-care decisions and suggested that these could be established in part by finding out what consumers wanted through community surveys. The 1989 White Paper *Working for Patients* went further and introduced market mechanisms as the most effective way to articulate people's demands and make producers and providers more responsive to consumer preferences (Flynn, 1992). This involved creating an internal market with purchasers being separated from providers. Under the NHS and Community Care Act 1990 hospitals now compete for contracts drawn up by the District Health Authority and GPs take on a pivotal role in choosing services for their patients. Such a market, it is assumed, will encourage doctors and managers to act in the best interests of the consumer.

As our study has shown, however, the notion of consumer sovereignty on which these policies are based seems to be problematic even when applied to private medicine – perhaps the archetypal example of health-care market. We found that subscribers had limited knowledge of their insurance policy and the costs of treatment and felt they lacked the competence to evaluate the skills of different consultants in order to make an informed choice. Rather than shopping around for the best deal they depended on their NHS GP to decide whether they should go privately and if so which consultant they should see. This suggests that patients will almost always be dependent on medical professionals and the issue is therefore how to regulate this dependence (Flynn, 1992) rather than trying to reduce the monopolistic position of these professionals in the name of consumer sovereignty.

Second, our research enables us to comment on the prospects for private medicine in the light of the recent health service reforms. One of the findings of our research was that people's perceptions of the waiting time for surgery under the NHS was an important factor in their decision to take out private health insurance. It may be that recent Government policy initiatives such as the *Waiting List Initiative* and the *Patient's Charter* may reduce these waits and make private health insurance less attractive to potential subscribers. According to Laing and Buisson (1990), however, there is as yet little evidence that NHS waiting times have been substantially reduced as a result of the *Waiting List Initiative*. Indeed they even question the extent to which it is a major problem. The introduction of self-governing NHS Hospital Trusts under the NHS and Community Care Act 1990 may however have some impact on waiting times as they will have little incentive to keep large waiting lists given that 'money will move with the patient' (Laing, 1989). Whether this is so or not, a wider recognition of the fairly short waits experienced by most patients could in the long term reduce the appeal of medical insurance.

Our research also highlighted the pivotal role played by NHS GPs in referring patients to the private sector. As a result of the recent reforms, these GPs now have a wider choice of provider units. The Health and Medicine Act 1988 has encouraged health authorities to set up NHS pay-bed units with standards of amenity equal to those in the private sector. Moreover, these are likely to increase as the new NHS Trust Hospitals consider their options for revenue generation. Faced with such a choice, GPs may refer fewer private patients to the private sector. On the other hand those GPs who have become fundholders under the 1990 Act may increase the number of patients they refer to independent hospitals. The need to relieve the pressure on their budgets may encourage them not only to get those patients with private health insurance to use it but to advise others to take it out (Laing and Buisson, 1990). They are certainly less likely than health authority purchasers to feel constrained to purchase diagnostic and surgical services from the NHS if the latter is felt to have provided an inadequate service for their patients. However, the cost of buying elective surgery from the private sector is unlikely to be attractive as long as surgeons' fees for private work remain at their current level.

The new reforms in the NHS appear, therefore, to be a mixed blessing for the private acute health-care sector. On the one hand, they may lead to an increase in the use of private hospitals by NHS purchasers. On the other hand, they may lead to a decrease in subscription to private health insurance despite the introduction of tax concessions for subscribers in the over-sixties age group. This downward trend may be encouraged by the recent marked increase in the cost of private insurance as described in Chapter 1. However, much will depend on the behaviour of employers. The recent growth in the private health insurance market, as we have shown, has mainly occurred because of an increase in the number of employers providing it free or at least paying for part of the subscription for certain members of their work force. Certainly, it has become one of the more common and attractive of the range of company perks and it could spread more widely to other sectors of industry. However, any expansion of this market will ultimately depend on whether companies are willing or able to foot the bill for increasing insurance premiums. Evidence (Boliver, 1991) suggests that some companies are becoming concerned about the so-called 'abuse' or 'overuse' of insurance by their employees and are taking steps to regulate this behaviour. There is also evidence that some companies have shelved plans to extend their schemes to the entire work force, others have opted for cheaper, more restrictive cover and some have started to exclude spouses and dependants (Spittles, 1992). Recent figures for 1991 show the number of subscribers fell for the first time in two decades. The number of subscribers paid for by companies fell by 3 per cent but the number paid for by individuals increased by 3 per cent. The net effect was a fall of 0.6 per cent.

While there is currently some uncertainty about the prospects for expansion of the private health insurance market in the UK, private health insurance companies do have the option of moving into a new and expanding market which could emerge as a result of the introduction of the Single European Market. One of the consequences of the Single European Market will probably involve a growth in the mobility of people within Europe which might lead to an increase in the utilization of cross-border health care (Leidl, 1991). Some uniform health insurance might be needed to cover patient use of health care in European countries where they are not insured. For example as Leidl states (1991, p. 1081):

> Also relevant to any consideration of health care financing is private health insurance: at least 50 million people within the community bought premiums worth 15bn ecus from 775 insurance companies in 1988. Private health insurance is used differently in member states; large changes may be expected when regulations for the insurance industry are harmonised.

Finally, our research has implications for how people are likely to view what we see as the Americanization of health care in the UK. As we have seen, our respondents supported the NHS in principle whether or not they had private health insurance and expressed a dislike of the prospect of a fully privately funded health-care system as in the USA. The recent reforms with the introduction of an internal market for health care, the development of GP fundholders along the lines of the US Health Maintenance Organizations and an enlargement of the role of the private sector can all be seen as part of a process of Americanizing health care in the UK (Navarro, 1991b; Hudson, 1992) and as such are likely to be viewed sceptically if not with outright hostility by the majority of the UK public whether or not they are in receipt of private health insurance. What our respondents wanted, like those who have participated in survey research (Taylor-Gooby, 1991a), was for the NHS to be improved even if it meant increasing taxes. Opting for 'a quick fix' based on policies imported from the USA while failing to increase the funding of the NHS substantially to keep pace with the demands placed on it by an ageing population is likely to mean that people will increasingly turn to private insurance and health care out of necessity rather than out of ideological conviction. If this happens, the principle of providing health care for all, free at the point of use, will have been sacrificed by default.

# REFERENCES

Allen, I. (1988) *Doctors and their Careers*. Policy Studies Institute, London.

Allsop, J. (1984) *Health Policy and the National Health Service*. Longman, London.

Allsop, J. (1992) 'The voice of the user in health care'. In Beck, E., Lonsdale, S., Newman, S. and Patterson, D. (eds) *In the Best of Health?* Chapman and Hall, London.

Annandale, E. C. (1989) 'The malpractice crisis and the doctor–patient relationship'. *Sociology of Health and Illness*, 11, 1–23.

Billig, M., Condor, S., Edwards, D., *et al.* (1988) *Ideological Dilemmas*. Sage, London.

Boliver, D. (1991) 'Getting caught in premium squeeze'. *The Guardian*, 30 November.

Bosanquet, N. (1988) 'An ailing state of national health'. In Jowell, R., Witherspoon, S. and Brook, L. (eds) *British Social Attitudes: The Fifth Report*. Gower, Aldershot.

Bowling, A. and Jacobson, B. (1989) 'Screening: the inadequacy of population registers'. *British Medical Journal*, 298, 545–66.

Bury, M. and Gabe, J. (1990) 'Hooked? The media's response to tranquilliser dependence'. In Abbott, P. and Payne, G. (eds) *New Directions in the Sociology of Health*. Falmer Press, Lewes.

Busfield, J. (1990) 'Sectoral divisions in consumption: the case of medical care'. *Sociology*, 24, 77–98.

Busfield, J. (1992) 'Medicine and markets: power, choice and the consumption of private medical care'. In Burrows, R. and Marsh, C. (eds) *Consumption and Class: Divisions and Change*. Macmillan, Basingstoke.

Butler, J. and Calnan, M. (1987) *Too Many Patients*. Aldershot, Gower.

Calnan, M. (1983) 'Managing minor disorders: pathways to a hospital and emergency department'. *Sociology of Health and Illness*, 5, 149–67.

Calnan, M. (1987) *Health and Illness: The Lay Perspective*. Tavistock, London.

Calnan, M. (1988) 'Lay evaluation of modern medicine'. *International Journal of Health Services*, 18, 311–22.

Calnan, M. and Williams, S. (1992) 'Images of scientific medicine'. *Sociology of Health and Illness*, 14(2), 233–54.

Central Statistical Office (1991) *Social Trends*, 21. HMSO, London.

Crawford, R. (1984) 'A cultural account of "health": control, release and the social body'. In McInlay, J. (ed.) *Issues in the Political Economy of Health Care*. Tavistock, London.

Day, P. and Klein, R. (1989) 'The politics of modernisation: Britain's NHS in the 1980s'. *The Millbank Quarterly*, 67(1), 11–23.

Dingwall, R. (1976) *Aspects of Illness*. Marten Robertson, London.

Dingwall, R., Fenn, P. and Quam, L. (1991) *Medical Negligence*. Centre for Socio-Legal Studies, Wolfson College, Oxford.

Doyal, L. and Elston, M. A. (1986) 'Women, health and medicine'. In Beechey, V. and Whitelegg, E. (eds) *Women in Britain Today*. Open University Press, Milton Keynes.

Dunleavy, P. and Husbands, C. T. (1985) *British Democracy at the Crossroads*. Allen and Unwin, London.

Elston, M. A. (1991) 'The politics of professional power'. In Gabe, J., Calnan, M. and Bury, M. (eds) *The Sociology of the Health Service*. Routledge, London.

Featherstone, M. (1987) 'Lifestyle and consumer culture'. *Theory, Culture and Society*, 4, 55–70.

Featherstone, M. (1990) 'Perspectives on consumer culture'. *Sociology*, 24, 5–22.

Ferriman, A. (1991) 'GPs cash in on reforms to buy services from own companies'. *The Observer*, 7 July, p. 3.

Finch, J. and Groves, D. (1983) *A Labour of Love; Women, Work and Caring*. Routledge and Kegan Paul, London.

Flynn, N. (1989) 'The "New Right" and social policy'. *Policy and Politics*, 17, 97–109.

Flynn, R. (1992) 'Managed markets: consumers and producers in the National Health Service'. In Burrows, R. and Marsh, C. (eds) *Consumption and Class. Divisions and Change*, Macmillan, Basingstoke.

Fraser, L. (1991) 'Private health crisis as thousands desert'. *Mail on Sunday*, 15 December.

Friedson, E. (1970) *Professional Dominance*. Aldine, Chicago.

Gabe, J. and Bury, M. (1991) 'Tranquillisers and health care in crisis'. *Social Science and Medicine*, 32, 449–54.

Geertz, C. (1973) *The Interpretation of Cultures*. Basic Books, New York.

Giddens, A. (1990) *The Consequences of Modernity*. Polity Press, Cambridge.

Giddens, A. (1991) *Modernity and Self Identity*. Polity Press, Cambridge.

Gillam, D. M. (1985) 'Referral to consultants – the NHS versus private practice'. *Journal of RCGP*, 35(270), 15–18.

Graham, H. (1984) *Women, Health and the Family*. Wheatsheaf Books, Brighton.

Green, D. G. (1985) *Working Class Patients and the Medical Establishment*. Gower, Aldershot.

Griffith, H., Rayner, G. and Mohan, J. (1985) *Commercial Medicine in London*. Greater London Council, London.

Haines, A. and Iliffe, S. (1992) 'Primary health care'. In Beck, E., Lonsdale, S., Newman, S. and Patterson, D. (eds) *In the Best of Health?* Chapman and Hall, London.

Ham, C., Dingwall, R., Fenn, P. T. and Harris, D. R. (1988) *Medical Negligence: Compensation and Accountability*, King's Fund Briefing Paper 6. King's Fund, London.

Hammersley, M. (1985) 'From ethnography to theory; a programme and paradigm in the sociology of education'. *Sociology*, 19, 244–59.

Hamnett, C. (1989) 'Consumption and class and contemporary Britain'. In Hamnett, C. *et al.* (eds) *The Changing Social Structure*. Sage, London.

Harris, R. and Seldon, A. (1977) *Not from Benevolence*. Institute of Economic Affairs, London.

Harris, R. and Seldon, A. (1987) *Welfare without the State. A Quarter Century of Suppressed Choice*. Hobart Paperback No 26. Institute of Economic Affairs, London.

Harrison, S., Hunter, D. and Pollitt, C. (1990) *The Dynamics of British Health Policy*. Unwin Hyman, London.

Higgins, J. (1988) *The Business of Medicine*. Macmillan Education, Basingstoke.

Higgins, J. (1992) 'Private health care sector'. In Beck, E., Lonsdale, S., Newman, S. and Patterson, D. (eds) *In the Best of Health?* Chapman and Hall, London.

Higgins, J. and Wiles, R. (1992) 'Study of patients who chose private health care for treatment'. *British Journal of General Practice*, 42, 326–9.

Hindess, B. (1989) *Political Choice and Social Structure: An Analysis of Actors, Interests and Rationality*. Elgar/Gower, Brookfield.

Hirsh, F. (1976) *The Social Limits of Growth*. Cambridge University Press, Cambridge.

Horne, D. (1986) Public Policy Making and Private Medical Care since 1948. PhD thesis. University of Bath, Bath.

Hudson, D. (1992) 'Quasi-markets in health and social care in Britain: can the public sector respond?' *Policy and Politics*, 20, 131–42.

Hughes, M. (1991) 'Fierce competition proves a headache for private sector'. *The Guardian*, 30 November.

Hunter, D. (1983) 'The privatisation of public provision'. *Lancet*, i, 1264–8.

Independent Hospitals Association (1989) *Survey of Acute Hospitals in the Independent Sector*. Independent Hospitals Association, London.

Judge, K., Solomon, M., Miller, D. and Philo, G. (1992) 'Public opinion, the NHS, and the media: changing patterns and perspectives'. *British Medical Journal*, 304, 892–5.

Klein, R. (1982) 'Private practice and public policy: regulating the frontiers'. In McLachlan, G. and Maynard, A. (eds) *The Public/Private Mix for Health*, pp. 95–128. NPHT, London.

Klein, R. (1989) *The Politics of the National Health Service*, 2nd edn. Longman, London.

Laing, W. (1985) *Private Health Care*. Office of Health Economics, London.

Laing, W. (1989) 'The White Paper and the independent sector: scope for growth and restructuring'. *British Medical Journal*, 298, 821–3.

Laing, W. and Buisson, R. (1990) *Laing's Review of Private Health Care 1990/91*. Laing and Buisson Publications, London.

Laing, W. and Buisson, R. (1992) *Laing's Review of Private Health Care 1991/92*. Laing and Buisson Publications, London.

Leidl, R. (1991) 'How will the Single European Market affect health care?' *British Medical Journal*, 303, 1081–2.

Loveridge, R. and Starkey, K. (1992) 'Introduction: innovation and interest in the organization of health care delivery'. In Loveridge, R. and Starkey, K. (eds) *Community and Crisis in the NHS*. Open University Press, Buckingham.

Mohan, J. (1986) 'Private medical care and the British Conservative Government: what price independence?' *Journal of Social Policy*, 15, 337–60.

Mohan, J. (1991) 'Privatization in the British health sector'. In Gabe, J., Calnan, M. and Bury, M. (eds) *The Sociology of the Health Service*. Routledge, London.

Mohan, J. and Woods, K. (1985) 'Restructuring health care: the social geography of public and private health care under the British Conservative Government'. *International Journal of Health Services*, 15, 197–215.

Navarro, V. (1991a) 'Production and the Welfare State: the political context of reforms'. *International Journal of Health Services*, 21, 585–614.

Navarro, V. (1991b) 'The relevance of the US experience to the reforms in the British National Health Service: the case of general practitioner fund holding'. *International Journal of Health Services*, 21, 381–7.

Nicholl, J. P., Beeby, N. R. and Williams, B. T. (1989a) 'Role of the private sector in elective surgery in England and Wales, 1986'. *British Medical Journal*, 298, 243–7.

Nicholl, J. P., Beeby, N. R. and Williams, B. T. (1989b) 'Comparison of the activity of short stay independent hospitals in England and Wales, 1981 and 1986'. *British Medical Journal*, 298, 239–42.

OPCS (1989) *General Household Survey, 1987*. HMSO, London.

Rayner, G. (1987) 'Lessons from America? Commercialisation and growth of private medicine in Britain'. *International Journal of Health Services*, 17, 197–216.

Roberts, H. (1985) *The Patient Patients*. Pandora Press, London.

Rose, G. (1982) *Deciphering Sociological Research*. Macmillan Education, Basingstoke.

Saunders, P. (1978) 'Domestic property and social class'. *International Journal of Urban and Regional Research*, 2, 233–51.

Saunders, P. (1986) *Social Theory and the Urban Question*. Hutchinson, London.

Saunders, P. (1989) 'Beyond housing classes: the sociological significance of private property rights in means of consumption'. In McDowell, L., Sarre, P. and Hamnett, C. (eds) *Divided Nation: Social and Cultural Change in Britain*. Open University, London.

Saunders, P. and Harris, C. (1989) *Popular Attitudes to State Welfare Services*. The Social Affairs Unit, London.

Saunders, P. and Harris, C. (1990) 'Privatization and the consumer'. *Sociology*, 24(1), 57–77.

Silvermann, D. (1984) 'Going private: ceremonial forms in a private oncology clinic'. *Sociology*, 18(2), 191–204.

Spittles, D. (1992) 'Private medical cover goes sick'. *The Observer*, 19 July, p. 38.

Stacey, M. (1976) 'The health service consumer: a sociological misconception'. In Stacey, M. (ed.) *The Sociology of the NHS*, Sociological Review Monograph 22. University of Keele, Keele.

Taylor-Gooby, P. (1986) 'Privatization, power and the Welfare State'. *Sociology*, 20(2), 228–46.

Taylor-Gooby, P. (1987) 'Welfare attitudes: cleavage, consensus and citizenship'. *Journal of Social Affairs*, 3(3), 199–21.

Taylor-Gooby, P. (1991a) *Social Change, Social Welfare and Social Science*. Harvester Wheatsheaf, Hemel Hempstead.

Taylor-Gooby, P. (1991b) 'Attachment to the Welfare State'. In Jowell, R., Brook, L. and Taylor, B. (eds) *British Social Attitudes: The 8th Report*, pp. 23–42.

Thorogood, N. (1992) 'Private medicine: you pay your money and you gets your treatment'. *Sociology of Health and Illness*, 14(1), 23–38.

Titmuss, R. (1969) *Commitment to Welfare*. George Allen and Unwin, London.

Tuckett, D., Boulton, M., Olson, C. and Williams, A. (1985) *Meeting Between Experts. An Approach to Sharing Ideas in Medical Consultations*. Tavistock, London.

*Which* (1991) 'Private medical insurance', June, pp. 322–33.

Wiles, R. (1993) 'Women and private medicine'. *Sociology of Health and Illness*, 15(1), 68–85.

# INDEX

**FINANCING HEALTH CARE IN THE 1990s**

**John Appleby**

The British National Health Service has embarked on a massive programme of change in the way it provides health care. The financing of the
Health Service is at the heart of this change and controversies over this issue
are likely to stay with us in the coming decade, whichever political party is
in power. This book explores some of the directions that the financing of
health care could take over the next ten years. For instance, will the
Conservative Government's stated commitment to a health care system
financed out of general taxation remain? Or, if the current reforms fail to
bring measurable benefits of any significance, will the political pressures to
take reforms even further lead to still greater changes in funding, financing
and operations? Will the state of the national economy necessitate further
reforms? Or might the reforms to date take an uncharted path, with some
unexpected outcomes?

For the senior student, academic or health care professional this book
offers an expert's view of the financing of the Health Service now and in the
future.

**Contents**
*New directions – Seeds of change – Past trends in health-care funding – The
right level of funding – A market for health care – Managing the market: the
US experience – Managing the market: the West German experience – Some
views of the future – Conclusions – References – Index.*

192pp      0 335 09776 6 (Paperback)      0 335 09777 4 (Hardback)

# PUBLIC LAW AND HEALTH SERVICE ACCOUNTABILITY

**Diane Longley**

This book examines the relationship between the processes of account-ability and management within the health service in the light of the recent National Health Service and Community Care Act. The author argues that health care is a social entitlement, to be moulded and allocated according to rational social choices and to be protected from becoming a commodity which is largely controlled by unaccountable market forces. Insufficient attention has been given to the potential role of law in the shaping of health policy and the management of the health service as a public organization. The arguments put forward here rest on a firm belief in a constitutional backcloth for the operation of all government and public services. The author calls for greater openness in health policy planning, in management and professional activities, the introduction of standards of conduct in health service management and for the establishment of an independent 'Institute of Health' to analyse and advise on health policy.

This important and timely book will be of interest to a wide range of students, academics and professionals interested in health service policy, politics and management.

*Contents*
*Diagnostic deficiencies: health policy, public law and public management –*
*Prescriptive dilemmas: accountability and the statutory and administrative*
*structure of the NHS – Cuts, sutures and costs: implementing policy and*
*monitoring standards – Patients and perseverance: grievances and resolution*
*– Sovereign remedies and preventive medicine: patient choice and markets –*
*Prognosis and preventive medicine: antidotes, tonics and learning – Bibli-*
*ography – Index.*

144pp      0 335 09685 9 (Paperback)      0 335 09686 7 (Hardback)

**HOSPITALS IN TRANSITION**
THE RESOURCE MANAGEMENT EXPERIMENT

**Tim Packwood, Justin Keen and Martin Buxton**

This book is the result of an evaluation commissioned by the Department of Health, that has given the authors exceptional access to the six acute hospital sites selected to pilot Resource Management (RM), over a three year period. Introduced in these National Health hospitals in 1986, RM is currently being implemented in all major hospitals. It was expected that patient care would benefit from better management of resources: management that involved the service providers and was based upon data that accurately recorded and costed their activities. This represented an enormous cultural change moving away from the traditional hierarchical and functional patterns of management.

The book draws upon close observation of the way in which RM has developed both locally and nationally, supported by interviews with the main participants, scrutiny of the documentation and specially designed surveys. It will provide an invaluable introduction to RM for all health service practitioners involved in management and to academics in health studies and public administration.

*Contents*
*Introduction – RM in context – Project planning and management – The implementation of RM – The RM process – The resource requirements of RM – Benefits of RM – Conclusions and implications – The organization transformed – Appendices – Glossary – References.*

208pp      0 335 09950 5 (Paperback)      0 335 09951 3 (Hardback)

## PLANNED MARKETS AND PUBLIC COMPETITION
STRATEGIC REFORM IN NORTHERN EUROPEAN HEALTH
SYSTEMS

**Richard B. Saltman and Casten von Otter**

The health policy debate in Northern Europe is increasingly focused on the question of introducing competition into publicly operated health delivery systems. The potential advantages and disadvantages of such a shift have come to dominate discussion among not only academics but also politicians, administrators, and now physicians and patients as well. 'Competition' has, not surprisingly, proved to be far from simple to implement in practice and many key questions surrounding its implementation in Northern European health systems remain to be answered. This book develops a new conceptual framework of 'planned markets' which will help policy makers and health service professionals to place narrow economic problems into the broader social and political context that they reflect. The authors present several different types of planned market models from Britain, Sweden and Finland and argue that the 'planned market' policy paradigm will strongly influence the future of publicly operated health systems throughout Europe.

*Contents*
*Part I: The search for a policy paradigm – The strategic crossroads – The emergence of planned markets – Planning and markets in the United Kingdom – Planning and markets in Sweden – Planning and markets in Finland – An analytic overview of planned market initiatives – Part II: The case for public competition – Civil democracy: a foundation for human service delivery – Administrative rationality in public sector human services – A theory of public competition – Planned markets in political perspective – Bibliography – Index.*

192pp    0 335 09728 6 (Paperback)    0 335 09729 4 (Hardback)